How to be a Brilliant Teacher

D0147639

This cheerful and accessible book is packed with direct and practical advice drawn from the author's extensive and successful personal experience as teacher-trainer, teacher and examiner. It sets out clear and practical guidelines to support and enhance your teaching skills.

How to be a Brilliant Teacher is aimed at teachers who want to develop their careers, or just be better teachers, by monitoring their own improvement. In order to do this, they may need to reconnect with theory, to consider their own practice explicitly, and to begin to see themselves as researchers. This book suggests how to get started. It is anecdotal and readable, and may be dipped into for innovative lesson ideas or read from cover to cover as a short, enjoyable course which discovers exciting principles in successful, practical experience.

Although a practical book, at its heart lie essential values about good teaching and learning. In particular it will seek to reintroduce teacher initiative and creativity and to reconcile these with the growing number of preformed strategies that the teacher has to work with. In exploring the issues faced by teachers it addresses many common anxieties and offers focussed solutions to them. Chapters cover:

- creative planning;
- managing learning, managing classrooms;
- issues in literacy;
- the paradox of inspirational teaching;
- differentiation;
- career planning and development.

If *How to be a Brilliant Trainee Teacher* helped you during your training, this book will continue to provide valuable support to you as you move forward in the profession.

Trevor Wright, University of Worcester, UK, has been a successful teacher for thirty years, and a trainer of teachers for ten years. Ofsted inspectors describe his school teaching as 'uncommon, exemplary, extraordinarily effective' and his teacher education work as 'inspirational'.

How to be a Brilliant Teacher

Trevor Wright

Illustrated by Shaun Hughes

Routledge
Taylor & Francis Group

LONDON AND NEW YORK

First published 2009
by Routledge
2 Park Square, Milton Park, Abingdon, Oxon OX14 4RN

Simultaneously published in the USA and Canada
by Routledge
270 Madison Ave, New York, NY 10016

Routledge is an imprint of the Taylor & Francis Group, an informa business

© 2009 Trevor Wright

Typeset in Sabon by Wearset Ltd, Boldon, Tyne and Wear
Printed and bound in Great Britain by TJI International Ltd, Padstow,
Cornwall

British Library Cataloguing in Publication Data
A catalogue record for this book is available from the British Library

Library of Congress Cataloging-in-Publication Data
Wright, Trevor, 1950–
  How to be a brilliant teacher/Trevor Wright.
    p. cm.
  1. Teachers–In-service training–Great Britain. 2. Effective
teaching–Great Britain. I. Title.
  LB1725.G6W748 2008
  370.71'55–dc22   2008011387

ISBN10: 0-415-41107-6 (hbk)
ISBN10: 0-415-41108-4 (pbk)

ISBN13: 978-0-415-41107-3 (hbk)
ISBN13: 978-0-415-41108-0 (pbk)

Contents

Acknowledgements

I would like to thank my colleagues in the Institute of Education at the University of Worcester for their many expert suggestions and contributions to the preparation of this book.

With thanks also to Shaun Hughes for the illustrations and to Caryn Thorogood for the index.

And thanks to Tim Coombs, who taught the symmetry lesson.

Introduction

Being inspirational isn't just luck, a happy accident of personality. It's tempting to believe that outstanding teachers are born with a rack of personality skills which deliver them inevitably into the classroom. They have charisma; they are minor pedagogical celebrities. Children are in awe of them; colleagues envy them; they are naturals. But this isn't necessarily the case.

This book sets out to show that excellent teaching is available to us all. You can learn to be inspirational. You can plan brilliance into your lessons. I hope to show that planning is where lessons live or die; that learning objectives aren't a bureaucratic menace but a major support for teachers. I want to argue that certain planning principles apply to all subjects and lessons and that by observing them you can palpably improve the atmosphere in your classroom. Behaviour, for example, has to do with lesson planning rather than rewards, sanctions and teacher personality. You need to create a mood to learn, and you can do this by becoming aware of the shape of your lessons, their rich learning moments, the directions they take. Many lessons offer a piece of learning and then work backwards from it; some lessons offer no new learning at all; most lessons concern themselves with the material to be learned rather than the pupils' need to learn it. The need to learn can be built in to every lesson. With dramatic results.

The inspirational teacher works from a dynamic tension which marries opposites. I hope to show you some ways of doing this, of stretching your practice across teaching extremes so that your lessons become active. I hope to redefine some old terms. What does *interactive* really mean? How does *pro-activity* differ from simple activity? And I want to offer you a new way of analysing classroom relationships, using the subtext of lesson exchanges to define learning conversations, and evaluating your teaching in terms of adolescents' continuing need for SFC – status, freedom and control.

I hope, in this book, to set formulae for brilliant teaching next to professional development and to show how research and CPD can enhance your teaching as well as your career. We work now in a post-Framework world and we need to take back our teaching and to return to creativity and individuality within the classroom. I hope that this book will suggest to you some ways of doing this.

Chapter 1

Getting better

We all have images of inspirational teachers. They come from many sources – from personal experience, from literature, from the media – and, if we set out to be teachers ourselves, those are often the models that we carry with us, especially at the beginning. Indeed, the most common reason given by young people for becoming teachers is that they were inspired by memorable individuals and now want to inspire others. More generally, the public has views about exciting teachers – they are eccentric, confident, creative and, of course, charismatic. There is an entire Hollywood sub-genre focused on teachers who make extraordinary breakthroughs in challenging circumstances. They make mould-breaking, institution-threatening relationships with young people which result in triumphant, filmic successes in sport, music and even, sometimes, poetry.

There's nothing wrong with idealism. The theme surrounding these icons is that of changing lives, and teachers entering the profession without that intention are at a serious disadvantage. The problem with the charismatic-inspirational model, however, is that it's exclusive. For one thing, it propagates a view of teaching based on performance. This notion of the good teacher – as an attractive front-of-class performer – has some value, and is common enough within the profession as well as outside of it; but it is limiting. It relegates the pupils to the role of awe-struck audience and fails ultimately to address the nuances of how learning happens. Moreover, as well as potentially excluding the pupils, this model excludes other teachers. The point of the maverick-genius teacher is precisely that he's not like the others. He has some sort of 'star quality' that his more mundane colleagues can only wonder at, envy or resent. Some people have got it; most people haven't.

Inspirational teaching is exciting and analysis of it tends to be excitable, too. If we calm down and look at it thoughtfully and systematically, we can reach another, more practical and authentic conclusion – that inspirational teaching isn't an accident of personality: it can be learned. Some individuals may arrive at it more intuitively (and so more fully and more quickly) than others, but we can all consider its various components and make organised and personal choices about improving our practice.

How do you get better at teaching? In a sense, of course, it just happens. The context in which you work is irresistibly evaluative; just about every transaction, every conversation you have in school provides feedback on some aspect of your performance. Some of this is bound to rub off, even if you don't notice it. But making sense of this incessant input, taking control of your practice and creating some sort of explicit system around your own development is important for your own peace of mind as well as for the development of your career. Understanding where you are and what you need to do is as calming as it is progressive.

The paradox of experience

You are a qualified teacher, successful and experienced. Of course, experience is a good thing; but it produces a conundrum in terms of development. The better you get at something, on a day-to-day basis, the more embedded it becomes. This is a problem teachers often meet when they begin to mentor other teachers, or to supervise trainees. They have to make their own practice explicit; they have to explain why they do certain things that, in all probability, they are hardly aware of. I remember trying to explain to my daughter, who was learning to drive, exactly how I changed gear – exactly when I moved each foot in relation to the other. I've changed gear quite successfully a few million times, but I couldn't tell her precisely how I did it.

To understand how to get better (and to recognise what you're good at) you have to deconstruct your own practice, to put yourself back into an analytical training mode. This is the switch you have to make. Let's consider some of the ways you can go about it.

Some key journeys

First, you could look at the *Development workshop* chart (Table 1.1) and mark your position on some of the lines. These are key

Table 1.1 Development workshop

From: **To:**

Limited activities ————————→ Inclusive differentiation

Nice activities ————————→ Genuine learning objectives

Subjective evaluation ————————→ Systematic evaluation

Administrating the lesson ————————→ Teaching the lesson

Extrinsic behaviour management ————————→ Intrinsic learning management

Teacher ————————→ Teacher-researcher

Skilled pragmatism ————————→ Overview

journeys in your efforts to be a better teacher. Some of these issues may be familiar; some may be less so; some may be so well integrated into your teaching that you've lost sight of them. The chart isn't exactly scientific, but it might at this stage help you to focus on some strengths and weaknesses in your work. As time goes on (perhaps as you read this book) you might return to the chart and track your movement.

Later chapters refer specifically and in detail to some of these continua but in the meantime a few are worth a preliminary glance. The overall movement, of course, is *from you to them* – from preoccupation with your own performance as teacher to the pupils' performance as learners. Inexperienced teachers, when evaluating their own work, will often comment on their own performance. They are preoccupied with issues such as pace, voice, explanation, questioning, task-setting, subject knowledge. These are all important, but it's interesting to compare them with the issues raised by more experienced teachers. They will evaluate pupils' learning rather than their own delivery. Indeed, *delivery* isn't part of teaching. You aren't a postman.

Another key change which you may need to make concerns how you see yourself and your work at the moment. As an experienced and successful teacher you may well be operating at a level of *skilled pragmatism*. You may have disconnected from aspects of your job which you associate with earlier experiences – with being new, even with being a trainee. These include addressing your practice explicitly, as we have said. You may need to stand back from the work and look at it through a new lens, because skilled pragmatism can deliver considerable success and is no small achievement; but at some point its usefulness expires. It will carry you so far at a given career stage and then you will need something else. This can sometimes, briefly, feel like stepping backwards.

It may involve, for example, building a more systematic evaluation practice. It may involve revisiting fundamentals such as lesson planning. It may involve collaborative working. It may even involve reading education theory. None of this is retrograde. I spent many years teaching pretty well without a word of theory in my head; but when I did read it, it made sense to me and improved my practice. Returning to your own development – teaching yourself teaching – is more meaningful the more you know. To take the simple example of observing other people teaching: student teachers do this. You may remember it. In September, three weeks into your training, you sit at the back of classrooms and are frankly amazed and largely bewildered by what you see. It tells you almost nothing, except that there's a lot of stuff that you can't do. Even a few months later – next summer, for example – that same activity has a meaning. Now you know what you're looking at. You may need now to switch into a new mode of being a teacher; to return to explicit and targeted learning. This does not deny your experience or achievements; on the contrary, it depends on them.

It's possible to subdivide this overarching model. In my experience, the single most powerful progression concerns *learning objectives*. I spent the best part of twenty-five years disliking and ignoring them, preferring to see myself as a creative and exploratory teacher and my lessons as places where surprising things happened. Even now I can't avoid gloom and despair when I attend a training event which begins with a PowerPoint slide of the intended objectives for the day. I just know that, six hours later, I will be shown the slide again and told that I've met them.

It wasn't until I began working with teachers and trainee teachers that I began to understand that all good teaching works from learning objectives and that, often, poor teaching is the result of planning which is based on activities rather than intended

learning. When you say, 'What are Year-7 going to do with this poem?' you should probably be saying, 'What are Year-7 going to *learn* from this poem?' This emphasis leads to teaching which is creative but focused. Of course, if your practice is secure you are already teaching to objectives, even if (like me) you don't recognise them. If the practice is implicit, progress will come best when you make it explicit and have a look at it. There is much more detail in Chapter 2.

Differentiation makes a rich and complex set of demands on teachers. The activity it requires seems infinite and it generates as much guilt and frustration as satisfaction. Most teachers believe that they aren't on top of it and that having three worksheets instead of one isn't the complete answer. *Learning styles* offers some solutions, but some of us are beginning to suspect that it's becoming a little overdone. In fact, differentiation is an emblem for the whole of the job; however hard you try, it's never enough. The *Every Child Matters* initiative in the UK seems to be asking for even more of it, in all kinds of difficult contexts. Perhaps it's time to confront this explicitly, to recognise what you're already doing (which is almost certainly more than you think) and the practical ways in which you can enhance it. There is a range of strategies in Chapter 6.

Evaluation is a key issue within any progress model, and there is much more information in Chapter 7. It's part of the process of making things explicit. Fundamentally, evaluation concerns the success of the learning. It needs focus: it can usually be covered by answering three famous questions about a lesson or a scheme of work: *What were they meant to learn? Did they learn it? How do I know?*

I see all sorts of evaluation practice. I'm amazed by apparently successful teachers whose evaluation, if it happens at all, is relegated to, 'I think that went OK...' as the children leave the room. At the other extreme, I've seen whole-school lesson-evaluation sheets which run to several pages of tick-boxes covering every possible behaviour of teacher and pupils. Frankly, what matters is the learning. You need to know what the learning was (so you need clear objectives); you need to have planned lesson components that will tell you whether it's taken place. Do you have a simple evaluation habit that asks the three questions about every lesson you teach? Do you have a lesson-planning format that indicates (as well as objectives and activities) your evaluation mechanisms? If you want to move forward, you probably should.

In the UK, we have moved through a Framework world. The National Curriculum has been extended into a secondary strategy with published learning objectives and teaching approaches. Much of this work is a genuine support to excellent teaching; but we now have to adapt to a post-Framework era. One of the disadvantages of the frameworks is that they appear to offer up entire curricula in a ready-to-teach form. We can use them; we can print off entire work schemes from the QCA; the planning has been done for us.

Of course, teachers need support; teaching has for decades been dogged by initiatives which have made new and bigger demands on teachers without offering any help in meeting them. The more recent frameworks and strategies can't be accused of this; they have generated lorry-loads of materials. This is helpful, but the problem is that, however carefully prepared, off-the-shelf materials cannot support individual creativity. Those charismatic teachers we remember didn't download their personalities from the Internet. Every lesson should feature somewhere a unique dialogue between teacher and pupils and we must stop regularly and consider whether *we are teaching lessons or merely administrating them*. Could somebody else, given the same materials, teach the same lesson? If that is more or less the case, then we are in danger of being de-skilled and de-professionalised by other people's systems. We do not need to abandon the frameworks (and, indeed, we can't), but we do need to reconnect with our individuality; and this (as so much else) happens not just in the 'delivery' but also in the planning.

In fact, I will argue throughout this book that *planning* is the most important thing a teacher does – that excellence grows from planning more than from exciting performance. Good planning builds learning, relationships and (incidentally) good behaviour. It might be interesting for you to consider where your own planning practice is at the moment. For one thing, the national strategies have created a new attitude to planning. There is certainly a lot more of it than there was ten years ago; but a good deal of it exists at work-scheme ('medium-term plan') level. Many teaching departments now offer plans which are followed by all and which were either garnered from published materials or created collaboratively by colleagues. Based as they are on lists of learning objectives, these plans are frequently content-driven, perhaps paying less attention than they should to the teaching pedagogy.

Additionally, it may be that you do less lesson planning than you used to. In my third (and final) decade of full-time teaching, I produced written lesson plans only when formally required to, which was very rarely. This is another paradox: nothing matters more than planning, but as we become more experienced, we do less and less of it. What we do do is often not at lesson-planning level, and focuses on subject content rather than pedagogy. Detailed planning at lesson level reconnects you with creativity; see in particular Chapter 2.

The final glance across the *Development Workshop* chart is at *behaviour management*. As a teacher trainer I deal with this every day. Nothing concerns new teachers more, and it crops up in every lesson feedback given to trainees by their school mentors. Advice given on these occasions usually falls into two areas. The first *is school systems*. The trainee teacher is struggling because she isn't consistent in her use of the school's rewards-and-sanctions policy, she shouldn't make threats she doesn't intend to carry out, and so on. The second area of advice centres on a subset of performance and relationship issues loosely known as *management skills*. This is all good advice and trainees need to hear it; but what is rarely commented on is the connection between the work and behaviour. In my experience of solving my own and others' management issues, it's usually the work that causes the problems; but this connection – which underlines

what's been called *intrinsic behaviour management* – seems not to be greatly discussed in school.

Let's consider further our attitudes to behaviour. Brilliant teachers, we might say, 'have pupils eating out of their hands'. We prize this ability very highly in the profession (and so do children, one of whose favourite complaints is, 'He can't control us...'). To what do we attribute this gift of good management? To good skills, to strong personality, to being likeable, to being firm-but-fair...

Children will say that these successful teachers respect them, don't talk down to them, understand them, are good at explaining, accept their genuine difficulties, are not boring. This looks at first glance like a list of personal qualities, traits you can take home and to the pub as well as into the classroom. Often, this is where the judgement of a teacher sticks; he has these knacks, the pupils like him, he's lucky to be the right person for the job. He's a natural. But if we consider this list a little more deeply, we can also see that a good many of these qualities are actually qualities of the work and can be *planned into the lesson*.

He respects us

Of course, this is a matter of personality and relationship. But it also manifests in the subject matter and conduct of the lesson. *Respect* includes taking time over the planning, choosing material that pupils will understand and respond to, planning opportunities for pupil discussion and opinion, showing genuine interest in their reactions, engaging with the content of what they have to say. Simple technical practices like including a range of question types or offering pupils choices of activity bring *respect* into the classroom. If a child volunteers an answer in a questioning session, how are you showing respect for that? If she offers an opinion that isn't the one you expected or hoped for, are you open to this? Do you engage with the content of what pupils say, or merely pass on until you get the right answer? Pupils know when they're being snubbed.

He doesn't talk down to us

Every teacher knows that it's fatal to patronise children, but this is much more than an issue of classroom manner. Pupils feel patronised by lesson content which they think is beneath them or by childish explanations. They like lessons in which their own opinions and predictions are sought and responded to. They are offended by teachers who don't explain (for example) *why* they're doing what they're doing. This sounds obvious, but are you planning such explanation into your lessons?

He understands us

How you explain tasks or new ideas to children reveals how carefully you've thought about them as learners. Have you anticipated their reactions and difficulties at the planning stage? Have you a *danger zones* section on your lesson plan? Have you thought about the need to recap? Understanding pupils is part of the *planning* process, not just a function of classroom manner.

He explains things well

This isn't about being a clear speaker. It's fundamental; it's about understanding learning. Like everything on this list, it looks like a personal quality deployed as a 'management skill', but actually it's a professional commitment to pupil learning. We will talk more about this in Chapter 3, but let's begin now by considering what's happening when something is explained well.

You explain well when you consider the explainee. I was recently given a set of directions by a helpful woman in a café. She told me with great accuracy and clarity how to get from the café to a school a few miles away. She explained it twice. When she had finished I thanked her and left, absolutely none the wiser.

She had no idea that I wasn't getting it and, as children frequently do when asked if they understand, I pretended that all was well. She had spoken to me from her own secure knowledge base with absolutely no sense that mine was different. She told me too much; she went into too much detail; she used words I couldn't understand (shop names I had never heard before), she gave me no help in remembering. I do see teachers doing this a lot. It's another teaching paradox: you have to be an expert on your subject but, when planning how you're going to talk to children, you have to imagine what it's like not to understand what you're hearing. This is actually quite difficult.

I was hopeless at science at school. I couldn't understand about atoms (and I still don't really believe in them). I tried very hard, but was always defeated. I remember the frustration now, and it's that memory – of not getting it – that I return to every time I plan a piece of teaching. Are you planning three or four ways of explaining key lesson ideas? Are you creating examples of and contexts for the new ideas that pay attention to pupils' own lives and experiences? Are you anticipating the difficulties of someone who has no idea what you're talking about? This is the core business of all teachers, not just the unlucky ones.

Boring and interesting

While we're translating from the adolescent, let's finally consider the two most important teenage words about teachers. The good teacher makes things *interesting*. The bad teacher is *boring*. In our efforts to improve, we must move beyond seeing these as matters of personality and recognise their pedagogical centrality. For us as teachers, there is nothing impertinent or trivial about these judgements.

Again, they sound like personal qualities. Indeed, *boring* is such a personal accusation that it's hard not to be upset by it and, often, we deal with this by resenting it. I used to ban the word from my classroom ('tell me *why* it's boring, and then I might listen…') but, if we begin to analyse it, we can systematically banish not the word but the quality itself.

I spend a good deal of time watching teachers and trainee teachers at work. After a couple of years of doing this, I noticed that I was bored. I was sitting at the back, looking at my watch and waiting for the finish; I began to feel guilty about this. Very often the lessons themselves were lively lessons; but this seemed to make little difference to my boredom. What was going on?

Of course, the lessons were designed for the children, not for me; our situations weren't identical. They were, however, analogous. What was happening to me was comparable to what was happening to them. It's interesting to compare their experiences with ours.

At the most basic level, I noticed that I could relieve the boredom by getting up and walking around. I could look at the children's work and talk to them; time would move much, much faster then. It's an obvious and basic thought, but I had the freedom to do this and they didn't. And I do less sitting in classrooms than they do. I will see, at most, two lessons in a day, whereas we expect children to do it all day long. Could you do that? And, at a slightly more subtle level, I have the *freedom* to stand up. I have the option. Even if I don't use it, the existence of the freedom itself, the sense of choice, is calming. Further, there is an element of status here. I am not in the lowest status position in the room. I have some control over what's happening to me. I chose to be there. Often, we expect children to sit still all day, with no status, freedom or control. They are adolescents, for whom there is little more important than status, freedom and control. It's a miracle that this ever works at all.

One underlying point here is that improvements of teaching which support the management of good behaviour – for example, by making lessons interesting and not boring – are also improvements to learning itself. It's fatal to make a distinction between planning for *interesting* and planning for *learning*, though I see this often. The teacher has a set of things to teach – some maths, some Shakespeare, some map work. He doesn't want the children to be bored so, having planned the meat of the lesson, he sets about decorating it with bits of interest. I have seen many worthy attempts at this. For example, he introduces quizzes. He tells some jokes. He downloads a *Who Wants to Be a Millionaire* template, complete with music and animations, and inserts some questions about perpendicular bisectors or pond-life. He even offers chocolate-related prizes.

This sort of thing can have some short-term success, but over a period the desperation of which it smacks becomes clear to the children and it soon becomes counter-productive. We tend to become uneasy with people who seek popularity and children are past masters at this. Perpendicular bisectors don't become interesting by association with jokes or prizes. Their only lasting hope is to be associated with the pupils and their lives.

We can begin to see *boring*, then, as an aspect of classroom planning. At its most basic, this underlines the need to plan structures and routines for choice, status and control. We can also plan for variety, which clearly offsets boredom, and so helps with behaviour, but which also provides ranges of challenging contexts within our teaching. It's possible (and really not even difficult) to create lessons which value adolescents and which are valued by them without losing control of the learning. *In fact, we can plan lessons that create a need to learn* (see Chapter 3). This is how learning and behaviour are married, and it begins to happen not in the classroom but in the planning.

Chapter 2

Creative planning

Creative teaching isn't the province of a few gifted eccentrics. It isn't even optional; all teaching is creative. It creates learning, routes to understanding, contexts, examples, analogies, narratives, purposes and metaphors. These are part of an ambitious but achievable checklist for brilliant teaching.

You connect back to creativity through planning, but planning, as we've said, is in an odd condition these days. There's a lot of it about; strategies set out its various levels and medium-term plans (in particular) are much thicker on the ground than schemes of work ever were. This is a good thing; but, on its own, this kind of planning is quite limiting.

For one thing, experienced teachers do less and less individual planning. They can manage without it, and they are formidably busy. For another, the UK secondary strategies and frameworks focus on three over-arching levels – long-, medium- and short-term planning – with little reference to the fourth: the lesson plan. These planning systems are largely based on learning objectives, listed appropriately for various age groups. This emphasis on objectives is potentially a very good thing indeed, but what it offers in the frameworks is an emphasis on the *what* and *when* of the curriculum. *How* learning actually happens in individual lessons receives much less attention.

Of course, this could be a good thing too, if it means that the creativity of teachers is not to be subject to top-down or bureaucratic planning systems. Just as all teaching can and must be creative, all planning must be imaginative. This is where individuality lives.

In fact, all plans – holiday plans, career plans, wedding plans – are imaginative. We fantasise about ideal outcomes; we guess at flashpoints and stress points and come up with contingent solutions. Lesson plans are the same. Teaching is triadic – it involves the teacher, the material to be taught and the pupils. This may be a truism, but I regularly look at planning which largely ignores the third element. This isn't so surprising. At the time of planning, only the first two – you and your subject matter – are present. You have to imagine the pupils, their reactions, their attitudes, their level of interest, their difficulties, and you have to plan in advance accordingly. You can't wait until the lesson goes wrong before deciding what you might do about it. More positively, you have to anticipate what the pupils will find interesting and create contexts and activities which will maximise this. We will come to some examples shortly.

As we said in Chapter 1, this at least means the imaginative process of seeing the new material through the eyes of someone who has never seen it, doesn't immediately understand it and isn't disposed to find it interesting. This isn't a portrait of every child, or even of a typical one, but planning that doesn't take account of it is, at best, only partially achieved and the resulting lesson will only partly succeed. One way of doing this is to remember what you were bad at when you were learning and consider how it felt and what might have helped. Another is to try out key lesson moments from your plan – key task setting, or explanations – on a friend who doesn't share your passion for your subject. Does she understand? Is she interested?

Let's go into some more detail and use some examples. We said earlier that good planning will consider not just the content and clarity of explanation but the pupils' route to understanding. It may use examples, analogies, parallels, contrasts and metaphors. If your planning currently stops at appropriate content well and carefully explained, now is the time to enhance your creativity.

I was recently watching a Year-8 history lesson. The subject was medieval doom paintings. I'm not a historian and didn't know that there were such things, but I found them interesting. This was partly because I have read medieval literature and know something about medieval attitudes to heaven and hell. The new information about doom paintings had somewhere to sit in my brain – next to Chaucer and *Piers Plowman*. This is an aspect of the learning theory we call constructivism; it's also common sense. In this respect, I had an advantage over the pupils. My mind had a place ready-shaped for the new ideas. I was thinking, as I sat there, of how the teacher could write a similar receptivity into her Year-8 pupils without expecting them to read *The Canterbury Tales* for homework.

She did well on her own. She projected one of the paintings and, rather than telling them about it, she gave them a list of artefacts to find. These paintings are complex and detailed, with many small images, some grotesque, some comic. The pupils enjoyed searching, as they had probably enjoyed search-picture books a few years earlier: they were on familiar ground; they were playing a game; they had structure and a focus (the list); they had an activity (the search), and the activity (a sort of DART; see Chapter 4) brought them very close to the painting. After ten minutes, they knew a lot about it. This was an enjoyable and productive activity.

The problem they had, however, was in really understanding the attitudinal context of the doom painting. It portrays in graphic terms the repercussions of Christian and (more to the point) non-Christian behaviour. Sinners are shown in hell, being tortured in a variety of entertaining ways. The painting is exhibited in church as warning. It is an instrument of social control.

Of course, children can be told this and they will accept it, as they will accept that Lima is the capital of Peru; but real teaching means that it will have a meaning for them, it will connect with their own experience, it will become memorable. In a fortnight, it will still mean something. It isn't so hard to make this connection at the planning stage. For example, in this case, children in a school already know about having their lives shaped by codes of conduct which are enforced via rewards and punishments, just like the doom painting. As soon as we made this connection, we were able to re-plan the lesson (for other groups), to clarify the objectives, to focus the activities and to achieve a new depth of understanding. We decided that, as well as knowing about doom paintings and about some other specifically historical aspects of context, which were of course already part of the medium-term plan, the children would understand how rewards and punishments could be deployed and communicated as components of social control.

We created a range of activities based around the simple comparison of the medieval context with their own lives. These included creative discussion: for example, in pairs they created their own school rules and then went on to expressing and enforcing those rules in words and pictures. They prioritised them; they created punishments which were appropriate in kind and degree. They considered varying options for publishing the rules and their associated punishments and rewards; for example, they considered expressing them through song, through jokes and through story as well as through written laws and, of course, through pictures. They thought about an audience that couldn't read. Thus, they became very close indeed to a personal understanding of the complex relationships within a society that used doom paintings to keep its people in check.

This process, essentially a process of comparison, allowed for wide-ranging and sophisticated exploration of concepts. I watched two or three of these lessons and heard Year-8 pupils considering (for example) the difference between school rules and medieval theology. Not only are school rules more trivial (obviously) but some pupils noticed that the relationships are different in kind. School rules and their sanctions are entirely man-made, whereas heaven and hell (presumably, to a medieval mind) are not. This contrast led to some real insights into the ways in which the medieval Church commandeered the divine for temporal purposes. Of course, the children didn't use this kind of language; but the comparison with their own experience enabled some new and impressive realisations. Similarly, a widespread discovery was that the medieval systems were essentially negative – more hell than heaven; this was helped by having them guess the name of this type of painting. Guessing and predicting activities are strong involvers and motivators. None guessed 'doom', of course; most of their guesses were less negative, and so they were intrigued by the uncompromising purpose of the term. Some of them concluded that modern sanctions systems are more rational and balanced than medieval ones; interestingly, though, not all agreed.

None of this happened spontaneously; the teacher proceeded through analysis, creativity, discussion and prediction, all of which were focused and structured. It all depended, however, on a single planning concept, which was the essential comparison of doom paintings with school rules, the constructivist attachment of the new learning to things the children already knew. Of course, some teachers will say that all of this discussion is ridiculously time-consuming. Children can understand doom paintings, their existence and function, within three sentences and we can quickly move on to the next fact about the Middle Ages. Such teachers will generate ten or twenty new pieces of learning within an hour. Lots of notes will be made, lots of information will be covered; everyone will think that a good job has been done. How much of this is roundly understood? How much will be retained in four weeks' time? Do you want to teach twelve things, of which eight will shortly be forgotten and the other four mixed up with each other, or do you want to teach two or three things well? In this history lesson, children understood a good deal more than simply that doom paintings existed. They had a sense of the medieval Church, its powerbase and its methods. They also had a sense of context and comparison; a sense, in fact, of historical process. This is one way of conjuring the third element – the children – into the planning process.

A Midsummer Night's Dream is a play about lords and fairies. Some teachers think that children love fairies (as they also apparently love the witches in *Macbeth*) but a little thinking about teenagers at the planning stage might take you in a better direction. Adolescents actually think that fairies are stupid. Their existence in the *Dream* confirms pupils' worst fears about Shakespeare. Even if they've never read or watched him, they already know that he's boring, difficult and pointless. This is the cultural context you've got to work with. That negative perception, as you plan your opening lessons, is at least as important as your knowledge of the Globe Theatre or Shakespearian comedy. Where is this in your plan?

This directly affects my selection of material and my learning objectives as I begin the play. Of course, children must understand it, but it's equally important to me that they enjoy it. Shakespeare was written for enjoyment; and you aren't going to get much out of the study if you hate it. These are learning objectives of equal significance – to understand and to enjoy. There's nothing trivial about enjoyment. In this case, if I had to favour only one, I'd choose *enjoy* every time.

At the beginning of the play, various lords with unpronounceable names talk about 'nuptials' in language no Year-8 pupil could possibly hope to understand, but then a family spat develops, in which a daughter's choice of boyfriend is rejected by her father. Her father thinks she should go out with somebody else; she refuses. Suddenly, we have a row which adolescents will recognise. They live with this sort of outrageous parental interference every day. My beginning lessons, then, will isolate this piece of tension and invite pupils into its familiarity. They will (for the moment) ignore iambic pentameter and the Globe Theatre. In fact, we will start the lesson by discussing family arguments with no reference to Shakespeare at all. That way we will reach an initial sympathy for Hermia, her plight and her possessive father.

Once again, this planning isn't just about Shakespeare and all the things I know about him (and the pupils don't); it's also about my best guess at teenagers and their lives. A new piece of learning is a new piece in a jigsaw puzzle; as you approach the puzzle, you have to find the hole where it will fit. You can't just bung it where it doesn't belong. If you can't see the receptor, you have to shape one before you try to add the new piece; or perhaps you have to reject the piece and choose another. And you certainly have to think about the cultural context of what you're asking them to do. They already don't much fancy learning calculus, because somehow they already know it's difficult. Older kids have told them that telling the time in French is a nightmare. You have to deal with this in your planning.

This constructivist fitting can be quite a subtle process. I recently watched a geography teacher explaining that a town can be categorised according to its function. We were in a town in South Wales which is a port, and the teacher began from that area of familiarity. He showed the children photographs of the wharfs and cranes and asked them what sort of a town they lived in. After some brief discussion it was agreed that things were imported and exported, on ships, and that Swansea, therefore, was a port. This was a good try at originating a piece of learning close to the pupils' own expertise.

It's interesting to consider in what ways this could have been even better. For one thing, there's the matter of *comparison*. It's a dull word, but I want to argue that comparison is a major asset, usually an essential, in defining terms. Consider the stickman.

You know very little about him until you see him in company:

Now you think that, possibly, he's a *small* stickman. Adding two or three more figures will confirm this beyond doubt. You can tell children that Wordsworth is very positive when describing London in the poem 'Westminster Bridge', but they really begin to see the point of this when you put Blake's extremely depressing sonnet 'London' next to it. Contrasting two things is much more than twice as effective as looking at one thing. In Swansea, the children see the cranes on the skyline every day. Looking at pictures of other towns with other features – for example, Birmingham, with no cranes but lots of factories – will help them to define function. The comparison, which may take up very little time, both sharpens and broadens definition. We are not just learning something about Swansea, we are learning about towns and how we talk about them. We are learning about geography.

This travelling from old knowledge to new understanding has to be subtly managed. This teacher tried; he showed them photographs of parts of their own town, but he insisted on defining the concepts for them. He asked them how they knew that their town was a port and the answer (which he quickly supplied) was that it exported and imported goods. He pointed at a photograph of the cranes to underline this.

This is a try at using pupil experience, but it could go so much further. The teacher is preoccupied with the definition of port and jumps to it almost immediately. This, after all, is the point of the lesson. In doing this so early, however, he is preventing the pupils from constructing their own understanding based on their own perception and experience. How do you know that the area you're driving through is an industrial area? Do you think, 'Hmmm. They're making a lot of things here; this must be an industrial area'? No: in fact, you're more likely to think, 'What a lot of lorries and factories. Not many houses. Definitely industrial.' Likewise, you know a port because you spot the cranes on the skyline, not because you're thinking about the economic activity which they represent. As a non-geographer, I am already equipped to make preliminary judgements about towns and their functions based simply on what I see. As a geographer, you have to consider how non-geographers like me think.

The point of using the pupils' home town to model a geographical concept is that they are already experts on it. All the teacher needed to do was to add prompt questions – what are those cranes *for*? – to build the new lesson concepts onto the pupils' prior knowledge. There may seem little difference between defining a port as a place that exports and imports things and defining a port as a place with ships and cranes. Indeed, the second definition may seem naive and incomplete, but it is the second definition that begins to build on pupils' existing understanding. The newer, fuller definition has a chance of bonding and staying because the brain is able to find a place for it.

Sometimes it's the language itself that provides the connection. A maths teacher is working on bisectors with a Year-7 group. There are perpendicular bisectors and angle bisectors. They appear to me (and I work at about Year-7 level in maths) to have little to do with each other, though obviously they come side-by-side in the work scheme. One thing they have in common is their name, but this point is never made in the lesson. The children probably know that *bi-* means *two* (they might recognise that a *bilingual* person speaks two languages or that *binoculars* have two eye-pieces); even this meagre reference would help them to understand the new word, to see the connections and, moreover, to see that maths, despite appearances, lives in the same language universe as the rest of us. Are you exploring and exploiting the language of your subject?

Learning objectives

In a Business Studies lesson, Year-10 pupils were designing holiday brochures. It seemed to be an active lesson; there was talk, cutting-and-pasting (literal and virtual), felt pens and computers. The material was bright and cheerful. But underneath the apparent bustle there was a kind of lethargy. Two boys did little more than copy a logo for about thirty-five minutes. Two girls copied and rewrote some advertising text. Slowly, pupils were producing amateurish versions of the real brochures that they were leafing through. It's quite a dispiriting process, I imagine, because it's perfectly obvious to everybody that your brochure will never look as good as the real one. I have watched (and taught) such lessons many times and it took me some time to realise what was going wrong. For her learning objective, the teacher had written *pupils will design a holiday brochure*.

Pupils don't need to be able to design holiday brochures, or websites, or posters. If they later decide to become advertising professionals, some training may become necessary; but in Year-10 this in itself is not a learning aim. *Design a brochure* is an activity, not a learning objective. It is almost certainly a worthwhile thing to be doing, but its value will never be fully exploited

until the teacher explicitly recognises its learning purpose. Lively, enthusiastic teachers who base their day-to-day work on *activities* can undergo radical improvement when they move from this to *objectives-based* planning and teaching. The change in focus and consistency can be dramatic.

Children don't go to school to do things; they go to school to learn things. Almost always, the best way of learning is by doing; but this doesn't mean that, of itself and implicitly, *doing* will automatically generate *learning*. The best classrooms are active, but those activities must be held together by the teacher's clear understanding of their purpose.

The term *learning objective* goes in and out of fashion. There are other terms, such as *intended learning outcome*, which some people take to mean much the same thing. And the astonishing discovery of the educational establishment that years of league tables and check-list management of the curriculum might have limited children's creativity could well lead to a backlash against learning objectives. This would be a shame, partly because it would represent a fundamental misunderstanding of what creativity is and how it happens in classrooms. We will talk more about this in Chapter 5.

Meanwhile, I offer the term *learning objective* because it might help to think of it as a physical object. The children walk into the classroom without it. An hour later (I call this 0–60) they leave, and they have the learning objective. Even now, after all these years, I picture this process as I'm planning. What will they leave the lesson carrying that they didn't come in with? It's a small but valuable object. And what will they remember tomorrow (0–24)? Or in a fortnight (0–14)?

Why are we designing holiday brochures? Let's say, for example, that we want pupils to understand something of how advertising texts work. An advertising text seeks to persuade. It chooses a target audience; it offers an image of its product that should attract that audience. It adopts all sorts of persuasive techniques to do this: it may exaggerate, or use euphemisms; it will select the information which it presents, including and omitting facts about the product with the express intention of persuading (rather than simply informing). If pupils can understand some of this, they will know more than they did about advertising. This is a worthwhile Business Studies objective and goes well beyond playing at travel brochures.

This sense of purpose has to underpin the planning and conducting of the lesson. For example, the teacher will obviously present examples of holiday brochures and the children will look at them; but the teacher must focus the work so that they are looking specifically at the persuasive intent and techniques, at the product image and target audience, because these are the learning objectives.

How can she do this? I want to revert to a point made earlier in this chapter. Comparison is your teaching friend. Show pupils two adverts rather than one. Let them look at a brochure page from *Club 18–30* holidays and another from *Saga* holidays. When they have them side-by-side, they can build detailed and structured comparisons. They can look at vocabulary, imagery, typefaces, layout, use of rhetorical questions. If you talk about the 'tone' of only one page, with no comparison, they *may* see what you mean; but if you place the shouty, matey tone of the young people's ad next to the calming, reassuringly expensive voice of the old people's, they will immediately see the difference. The comparison of the two may not be the main purpose of the lesson, but it will certainly build the appropriate concepts.

They can then make decisions about their own brochures through a structured planning activity which requires of them their intended age group, holiday tone and mood, price bracket, location, layout and so on. They must decide on these before beginning. Rather than simply leafing through brochures and copying them, they have garnered a small checklist of techniques which you have prompted them towards, based on your learning objectives. The lesson now hangs together around clear central ideas. The pupils have a sense of purpose and process. You know what they're learning. Their finished brochures should enable you to evaluate it. And the concepts they've learned may be transferred in the future to other contexts.

The lesson which presents the activity *design a brochure* as a learning objective lacks a sense of direction. It may get the job done; it may generate a whole wall-display of pretend brochures; but if you aren't clear what the learning is, you can't check whether it's happened or how it fits into the learning curriculum. Even behaviour management is influenced, fundamentally, by lesson design. The children copying out holiday ads with little sense of why or what they're looking for will quickly become bored. The children with focus and deadline will get on with the job. They are working within a structure generated by a true learning objective – *pupils will understand the persuasive intention of a holiday brochure. They will understand the concepts of target audience and product image.*

Let's just consider this learning objective for a moment more. As presented above, it conforms to one of the three conventional objectives types – skills, understanding and knowledge. Most objectives can be expressed as *children will know* or *understand* or *be able to...*, though I would always add that the notion of incremental learning can be included with words like *more* or *better (children will know more about*, or *understand better...).* But the objective presented above is actually several objectives. One of the key skills in devising learning objectives is understanding that they are staged and that often one objective is actually several. The careful teacher takes account of this in her planning.

You want pupils to understand dramatic irony within a scene from *A Streetcar Named Desire*. This is fine, but you must understand that there are at least two learning objectives here. They need to know what dramatic irony is *before* they can see it in a particular play. Teachers who disentangle these learning stages and deal with them systematically are supporting learning development and visibly improving their own practice. The poor teacher comes upon the dramatic irony as it crops up in the play, pauses and defines it (*Look at this; this is what we call dramatic irony...*) and then moves on. The children are expected to simultaneously learn a new idea, new language for it (not the same thing – why is it *called* this? Why is it *ironic*? What is *irony*, in fact?) and see how it works within a play which they're studying. There are at least three pieces of challenging learning all vying for their attention here. Of course, the play (in this example) provides the context for the learning; you can't have one without the other; but there are stages that you must take account of in your planning. This begins with the learning objective. Compare:

> Children will understand dramatic irony in the opening scene of *Streetcar*.

with:

> Children will understand dramatic irony.
> They will understand how it works in the opening scene of *Streetcar*.

Splitting your objectives like this invites you to plan lessons which take helpful account of the learning stages. For example, in this lesson you might begin with a discussion of dramatic irony in *Eastenders* or *Home and Away* (soap operas love dramatic irony). You might do some group role play around the notion of dramatic irony. Following starters such as these, you would reach a key transition point where you took stock with the class of what they've been doing. You would consider what the *Eastenders* work had to do with the role play. You would work with them towards the sense that these were dramatic situations where the audience knew more than some of the actors on stage. So we move towards a definition of dramatic irony and an understanding of its effects. Only when we are certain that we have grasped this do we turn to our play, *Streetcar*. We carry our new learning into a fresh context. We are confident rather than confused.

There are many advantages to this stepped-objectives approach. It encourages a lesson build which is progressive. It creates lesson beginnings which work because they are close to the pupils and their experience (they don't know much about irony or *Streetcar*, but they are experts on *Eastenders*). It therefore creates new concepts within familiar and confident contexts. It creates a lesson shape which is increasingly challenging from a comfortable beginning. It moves (often) from the personal to the formal and from the concrete to the abstract. All of this is achieved simply by working from clear objectives and splitting them if necessary.

Some myths about objectives

It's very difficult to think them up

The objective is what the children learn. If this isn't the basis of your teaching, what is? But objectives don't have to sound grand, general and academic, and the most useful ones don't. You may discover your objectives within subject frameworks or medium-term plans, but they almost always need rewriting. They are your planning friends, not an additional burden; but to become so, they need to be local, specific and down-to-earth. You are their boss, not the reverse. *Children will have a better understanding of German grammar* isn't a meaningless objective, but it falls a long way short of telling you what to do on a Thursday afternoon. *Children will understand one way of forming imperatives* may sound less impressive but it's actually much more helpful as a basis for planning and evaluation.

Similarly, compare:

> They will understand a writer's methods and techniques.

with:

> They will see how and why Causley uses similes in the poem 'Timothy Winters'.

The first sounds reassuringly official but the second is your own and is offering you help in planning your lesson activities. A good compromise is to write both objectives (the second exemplifies the first), but if you only want to write one of them, the second type is the one to go for. With learning objectives, small is beautiful.

Of course, given what we've said about staged objectives, the best formulation is really:

> They will understand similes.
> They will see how and why Causley uses them in the poem 'Timothy Winters'.

They spoil spontaneity

They provide focus and continuity, but any lesson can undergo radical changes on the day. The ones that do are sometimes the best ones. If the lesson is a journey, the objectives are the destination. You can't plan without them, but of course in the event you may find yourself taking a detour or stopping to admire an unexpected view.

You can teach perfectly well without them

This can never be true – how can you teach without planning for pupil learning? – but it's interesting to consider why it gets said. Experienced teachers say it; I thought it myself for many years. I was happily hostile to the whole concept; I was a creative teacher who enjoyed the unexpected. But my pupils were learning, and they were learning because, of course, my planning was based on implicit learning objectives. I knew why I was doing what I was doing, as you do. Good teaching often gets done by teachers who are using objectives implicitly. Their teaching will become even better when they recognise that they are already using objectives and begin to plan explicitly around them.

You have to write them on the board at the start of every lesson

You should always know and plan from your objectives, but your lesson plan might not require the pupils to know them from the start. Lessons may often have an air of exploration; pupils are working towards the objectives, not recovering from an initial definition of them. In fact, the mechanistic reputation of objectives may stem from the rigid lesson shape which demands their initial publication on the board and final evaluation where pupils dutifully report at the end of the lesson that they have, indeed, learned what they should have. Sometimes, if the lesson is a story, the objectives are the hidden treasure. Sometimes, having the pupils guess the objectives which have been threaded invisibly through the lesson is the best kind of evaluative plenary.

You don't need them with sixth-formers

Of course, post-16 teaching is different. The pupils are volunteers; they love the subject; they love learning; you don't need to plan systematically; all you need is a gas fire, some marshmallows to toast and a schooner of medium-dry sherry to sip as they read their essays aloud in the darkening afternoon.

You may have noticed that this is a fantasy, but it's not an uncommon one. Post-16 teaching requires all of the planning, structure and focus of the rest of your work. It certainly requires local and specific learning objectives, and here as elsewhere they are a support to collaborative and focused teaching. The line-by-line approach, working jovially through the textbook, is especially tempting and especially unproductive at this level. Clear objectives provide structures for lessons which generate discussion and understanding. A brilliant teacher never enters a classroom to teach chapter 17 for no other reason than that she taught chapter 16 yesterday. Chapter 17 has a new piece of learning, a new concept and a new lesson to be built around it. Of course, post-16 teaching offers a new range of opportunities – the possibility of smaller groups, of more independent study, of more adult content. And post-16 lessons should be largely discursive; nearly every lesson is a conversation; and this puts speaking and listening where it should be – at the heart of your teaching (see Chapter 4). But these conversations need as much planning as all of your other lessons, and there are more similarities between post-16 and lower-school teaching than there are differences.

Chapter 3

Managing learning, managing classrooms

We have all been influenced by the Hollywood teacher. He strolls into unpromising classrooms, he is excitingly dressed, his unruly adolescents (abandoned by all the other teachers) show him some grudging regard, perhaps because he wears an earring and may be about to swear. Within hours he is their champion and they are living new and productive lives, forming choirs and competition-winning hip-hop dance troupes.

It's hard to find anything right about this model of the brilliant teacher but it's a pervasive one, reflecting the anxieties of the profession and individuals within it. In terms of the management of behaviour and learning, this is a pernicious template and young teachers may take months or years to recognise its limitations. As we've said, pupils are not audiences and teachers aren't performers.

The language around the running of classrooms is interesting. We used to call this *discipline*, and this is still a popular idea in sections of the tabloid press. It's a useless term and we should be glad that it's disappeared from professional discourse. It reflected a societal and cultural attitude which has vanished and it has nothing to do with learning. The Hollywood maverick was an understandable reaction against it. The term *behaviour management* has replaced it and this is certainly more accurate in describing the skills and techniques which we use to make classrooms work. It recognises that running a classroom is a managerial activity, complex and demanding. Management is reciprocal, after all, whereas discipline, even in its oxymoronic form of 'self-discipline', is a top-down business.

What *behaviour management* fails to take account of, though, is the essential connection between children's behaviour and their learning. In this chapter I want to use the term *learning management* instead. I want to make the point that well-planned lessons with clear objectives and creative and constructivist structures will improve behaviour, and that poorly planned lessons will guarantee unhappy classrooms, even for the charismatic teacher, who will have to work harder and harder to compensate. This chapter should be read in conjunction with the whole book, because the management of learning and behaviour are not separate issues. In the end, improving behaviour does not depend either on personality or a set of so-called *management skills*. It is intrinsic to good teaching and thus dependent on good planning, and you shouldn't read this chapter without at least reading Chapter 2 first.

Motivation, motion and motive

Another popular term within this area is *motivation*. It's an interesting word, though it tends to get hi-jacked by the charisma brigade. *Motivational speakers*, after all, are performers; they stand on stages and rouse audiences into fervours about sales figures or Christianity. So teachers *motivate* by the strength of their personalities and performance; but this, as we've seen, is a misleading view of what teaching actually is.

But motivation remains very important. After all, if children are working, they are probably behaving, so management problems are solved. And there are only two reasons for children not to be working in your classroom: either they can't, or they don't want to. If we can overcome these two barriers, we have solved our behaviour problems. Motivation concerns the second of the two and it deserves some serious thought. It is, of course, connected verbally not only to the idea of *movement*, but also to the idea of *motive*. Children move when they have a reason.

When did you last learn something? Clearly, in one sense, you are learning all the time. Perhaps you are learning as you read this book. If you try a new dessert in a restaurant you are learning about a new dessert. If you have to visit someone's house for the first time, you are learning the way there. But these are choices you have made. And you like learning.

The last thing I had to learn was how to configure a broadband router. I had to buy a new one and making it work with my Internet Service Provider and my home network proved a nightmare. It took several days of frustration and swearing, trying to make sense of information clearly written for people who already understood it. I had no choice; I had to stick with it because I needed my router to work. No part of this was enjoyable. If I could have got out of doing it, I would have. But my motivation was irresistible.

In all seriousness, I invite you to pause for a moment and remember when you last undertook a piece of formal learning like this, a piece of learning that was forced upon you from outside. I ask you to remember what motivated you and how you felt about it. And I ask you to consider that we expect adolescents to do this all day every day, to learn new things for no other reason than that we tell them to.

Of course, some pupils will learn because they like learning. Others may well be prepared to learn just because we say they must. The other ones, who aren't so easily motivated, are the ones we need to consider, not only because they're the ones who cause us trouble but because they are actually revealing the weakness in our teaching.

Certainly, one source of motivation is trust. If we have clear and progressive relationships with children they may be prepared to learn because we tell them that it's a good idea and they accept that we are usually right. But how is this trusting relationship built up around the area of motivation? How explicitly are you addressing motivation in your lesson *planning*? What are you saying to pupils about it? At its simplest, this can be a matter of explicit and extrinsic statements, but how often are you making them? Are you writing them into your lesson plans?

Let's consider the statements we make to children about behaviour and motivation. It's interesting to consider how close to the actual work they are. I want to argue that the most distant statements are the least effective. These are statements about sanctions and rewards policies and, literally, they have nothing to do with the work. They are all-purpose comments of the 'You must work, or else…' or the 'If you're good, you will be rewarded…' variety. Such statements and the policies behind them are necessary and valuable, but we have to pause and consider why this is so. As raw motivators they are quite weak. Disaffected adolescents are not greatly impressed by merit marks or by threats of detentions which they probably won't turn up to. What is valuable about these systems, however, is that they can be used to depersonalise your attitude to bad behaviour, to remove stress, to counter competition and confrontation.

You aren't alone in a classroom. You represent local and national institutions and they are there to support you. Invoking school sanctions is one way of reminding pupils where the power lies – not with the strength of your personality and conviction, but with bigger, established systems which are harder to resist. They generate consequences for poor behaviour which don't originate with you or depend on you. You should remember this when invoking sanctions: it isn't a personal business. You aren't desperately lobbing threats across the classroom. You are saying, perhaps literally, 'If you continue with that behaviour, you and I know that there will be consequences. You know what they are. The choice is yours.' The pupil's offence isn't against you; it's against the school, and the school will deal with it. There's almost never any need for confrontation in a classroom built around this kind of dialogue. It can (and should, at best) be a quiet dialogue. The power lies with the inevitability of the consequences, not with the thundering of the teacher; and the choice lies with the pupil. I have said on quite a few occasions, quite quietly, 'I've asked you to move. You're saying you won't move. You do understand that if you won't do as I say, you are bound to be in quite serious trouble?' At that point you walk away. If the pupil doesn't move, you quietly begin to invoke the consequences, in terms of contacting senior staff. You send a note. But usually it isn't necessary.

Next to these distant, extrinsic statements are a range of extrinsic motivators which are a little closer to home. They are effective, but I'm surprised at how rarely I see teachers use them, or how infrequently they are reinforced once established. These are statements of the 'You need to listen to this, or your homework will be harder for you...' variety. Here the pupil is offered a straightforward, procedural reason for working. Personal, work-related benefits may accrue from getting on with it. Similar statements focus around assessment issues. 'If you do this, you will be able to raise your level...' or, 'If you don't do this, you won't get above a grade D' can offer genuine motivation, especially to older pupils. These statements are far from ineffectual, but often teachers take them for granted – surely pupils already know what they're working towards? They may or they may not; but they certainly need reminding, and these reminders need to be proactively planned into your lessons, forming part of your task setting. At their best, such comments underwrite the whole lesson, explaining each activity in terms of its purpose and links to the others, and so helping to make powerful learning transitions.

Proactivity

This point about being proactive is crucial. The term is sometimes written off as meaningless jargon, a fancy way of saying 'active'. It's neither. The difference between reactive and proactive management is vital in terms of classroom mood.

Let's drop into a chaotic classroom. Children are being naughty and the teacher is hurling threats at them, or trying to reason with them. He's telling them off about their attitudes; he's already lost. They are in charge and they are organising his behaviour, rather than the reverse. The motivation, the reasoning, the explanation of *why* they should work, has to come *first*, while you're still running things. It is part of your planned communication, instigated by you, not by them. This is why imaginative planning is so important, and behaviour management is part of it. Statements relating to motivation need to be offered *positively, as part of your pre-planned dialogue*, so that you are in charge, not the children. Defensive statements offered in reaction to bad behaviour are bound to fail. How often do you say, 'We are going to do this now *so that you can understand how to do the best possible job* with your coursework', or, 'Knowing this *will be really useful to you* in the following ways...'? What matters isn't so much the quality of these motivational explanations but the timing of them. Get in first, and then you can be positive. Offered too late, they are simply confirmation of the fact that you've lost control.

Why does an eleven-year-old boy need to know what a perpendicular bisector is? What thought are you giving to this in your *planning*? Telling him that before he starts is strong, and telling him off as he falls off task is weak. If I hadn't already known *why* I had to learn about my router, I would have given up and left the room. If I'd been prevented from doing that, I would have shouted at someone.

The fact is, however, that even these extrinsic motivators are still some distance from the work itself. They have to be invoked, rather than being present in the classroom atmosphere. We become stronger motivators when the motivation is intrinsic, because intrinsic motivation values both the work and the children and connects the two.

In a general sense, of course, intrinsic motivation may be said to concern making the work interesting. This involves finding material which is appropriate to the adolescents we're teaching, finding ways of exploiting that interest, finding ways of explaining that don't patronise, and so on. We talked about some of these 'making it interesting' issues in Chapter 2. 'Making it interesting' isn't just a case of being lively, telling stories and cracking jokes. At least, it involves constructivist sensitivity to the pupils' preparedness for learning, as we discussed earlier. But let's now consider this business of motivation in more depth and see how we can create a simple lesson structure that will generate the need to learn.

The need to learn

I would have abandoned my new router if I could; but I couldn't. My motivation was inescapable; I had to get on the Internet. The need to learn was absolute and so I persevered. In what sense do your pupils *need to learn* what you're teaching them? In what sense are you explaining this to them? More to the point, in what ways are you creating lessons which of themselves create a need to learn?

Let's consider three lesson shapes. These are represented by the three graphs in Figures 3.1, 3.2 and 3.3. The first shape is a flat line. This is a common enough sight in a classroom; the learning attempts to move evenly from start to finish. This is a lesson based on a process; it's a lesson based on getting on with it. You're doing your coursework; you know what you've got to do; I'll come and see how you're getting on. Or, we're working together through exercises, or a piece of text. There are no high or low spots of learning in such a lesson, just a sort of homogeneity. It lacks what we often describe as *pace*, but work gets done.

Such a lesson struggles to introduce new learning. Let's look instead at the second graph – Shape B. This is extremely common; you've sat in this lesson hundreds of times. The Hollywood teacher is quite keen on this shape as well. He walks into the room and announces today's subject, often in the form of one word. 'Today we're going to talk about DEMOCRACY' he'll say, writing on the board in those enormous letters that American film-star teachers go in for. 'Who knows about DEMOCRACY?' he asks. 'Who can tell me what DEMOCRACY is?' He casts charis-

Figure 3.1 Lesson Shape A: flatline lesson.

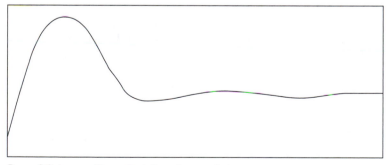

Figure 3.2 Lesson Shape B: define-then-apply lesson.

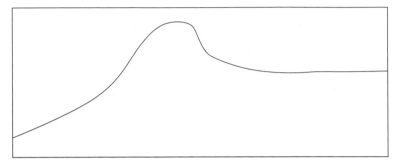

Figure 3.3 Lesson Shape C: need-to-learn lesson.

matically around the room as his delinquent students struggle and, despite themselves, become strangely fascinated.

I've taught this lesson dozens of times. I see it almost every day. 'Today we're going to talk about similes! Who knows what a simile is? Anyone heard of similes?' You can substitute any new piece of subject learning. As a beginning, it isn't without virtue. This is a teacher who (unlike Shape A) is moving students on by using a defined learning objective. He is telling students what the objective is. He is also quite properly trying to check what they already know. So what's wrong with this?

We have argued that planning is imaginative and part of the imaginative process is foreseeing pupil reaction. One problem with this kind of opening is that the questions are irritating. No, actually, I don't know what a simile is. If I did, you wouldn't need to tell me. Why are you asking me, when you're going to tell me anyway? Why are you making me feel stupid for not knowing? Don't you know what I know? Just get on with it. Tell me about the flaming similes.

More to the point, in terms of motivation this is a weak shape. The new learning is at its most explicit at the beginning of the lesson. The rest of the lesson consolidates and perhaps evaluates that learning. There is a simple logic about this, obviously. But the experience of such a lesson is not strongly motivating. We feel that we're moving backwards, not forwards.

This common lesson shape mistakes definition for learning. The explicit teaching happens at the beginning and is based on a definition. *Democracy* or *attrition* or *simile* mean something. When we know what it means, we know what it is and we can apply it. We define, then we apply. It makes a sort of sense until you consider the limitations of learning by definition. In reality, we don't learn like that. How many words have you actually learned from a dictionary? We learn when we need to learn. Let's consider Shape C as a simple template for a lesson which builds in motivation by creating that need.

One of the best lessons I have ever seen was a Year-8 maths lesson. The teacher entered the classroom and drew a vertical line down the middle of the whiteboard. He then drew a small cross to one side of the line. The children watched him as he paused; then he drew another identical cross opposite the first, on the other side of the line. After another pause, he drew another cross, somewhere above the original cross, and offered the board marker to the class. A few hands went up. A volunteer took the marker and drew the fourth cross, exactly opposite the third one. And so the lesson went on for some minutes, the children increasingly active. Not a word was spoken.

Although a maths lesson, and a very elegant piece of teaching, this was also a lesson in literacy. It was about *symmetry*, of course. It worked almost perfectly for a number of reasons. It had a single, clear and focused objective; it was highly interactive; it generated the need for a piece of learning and then met that need.

If you begin your lesson with the word, the concept, the key learning, you can only travel backwards. The lesson becomes a

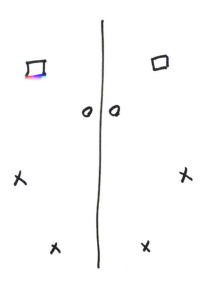

retrospective. Instead, plan your lesson to *move forward towards the key learning moments*. After six or eight minutes drawing crosses and then circles in varying positions and colours, the maths teacher started a discussion about the children's decisions. Why had they drawn what they had drawn? They explained to him, using words like *opposite*, *mirror*, *same place*. They reached a point where, in order to continue the conversation, they needed an appropriate word. The teacher, having created the concept, having explored it through activity, having generated the need for the word, finally supplied it. The pupils, rather than being bored, mildly interested, passive, were actively grateful. They were relieved, because they needed the word and now they had it. When they went home that night, they would be able to tell anyone who asked them what symmetry was. The concept comes before the word and creates the need for it.

This simple format – Shape C – can be applied to most lessons in most subjects and can transform your classroom. After seeing it, I created a corresponding English lesson in which pupils would learn something of the power of similes. I draw on the whiteboard a large egg shape and I write the label *head like an egg* with an arrow to it. I then add a feature – for example, I draw a large, red eye and write *eye like a tomato*. One by one the pupils come to the board and add features (*ear like a biro*, *spots like baked beans*). This is a comical lesson and every child can have a go.

After this, of course, we discuss the character we've created. He isn't beautiful. He certainly isn't symmetrical. We might name him. We might write a class poem about him. What we certainly do is reach the moment of discussion of what we've done when the pupils need the word *simile*. We then spend time on the word, including on its spelling (since only six people in England can spell *simile*). We define it together, and this includes understanding why you might use it.

There is, of course, no point at all in teaching children what a simile is if they don't have some sense of its effect on them as readers. Why is *spots like baked beans* better than just *spots*? Here we have spent twenty minutes laughing and thinking up increasingly outrageous (and occasionally obscene) similes. We now *know* from our experience that similes liven things up; they can, we now know, make things funnier. We have discovered this in creating them. We haven't just been told it; we know it. Next we read a poem which features similes and we can recognise and talk

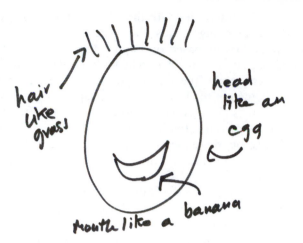

about the effects of those similes, because similes and their effects are already ours.

This, then, is a simple and adaptable lesson shape. Decide on the learning objective. Decide on the opening activities (we could call these 'starter' activities) in which the children will explore the objective conceptually before receiving the full definition. This is constructivist teaching; you are creating the receptor for the new learning before dropping that learning into place. The explicit teaching, which may be one-third of the way through the lesson, is carefully planned to draw the learning from the opening activities and place it out in the open where everyone can look at it and talk about it. The conversation will be based on what the children have already found out, combined with what the teacher knows about it.

Transitions

Any teacher knows that learning should be active and exploratory, and the shape outlined above factors activity into the lesson. Active and interactive classrooms are rightly favoured by all new and current prescriptions for good teaching. Perhaps, though, it's time to take stock of where this emphasis has delivered us to.

Teaching based on such principles is naturally planned around pupil activity. What are they going to do? It's not uncommon for lesson plans, when they exist in written form, to amount to a series of activity descriptions. In the UK, secondary subject frameworks set out planning in this way. The famous 'three (or four) part lesson' is a recipe based on pupil activity – the 'parts' are, in fact, pupil activities. This is excellent, but there is an emphasis here which can move the teacher to the role of administrator, whose job is merely to devise, explain, supervise and evaluate a series of activities. That is what lesson plans very often look like. The moments between activities are barely considered in the planning. In discussion, these moments are often seen, at best, as 'task-setting' moments. Often, the intention is to get through them as quickly as possible.

Teachers are right to be diffident about lengthy bouts of teacher-talk. Three minutes is enough for a lesson beginning. Children aren't good at listening; they learn better when active. But the teacher has a role which goes beyond facilitation and this involves talk which is much more than task setting. One advantage of the lesson shape we're talking about is that pupils can be set quickly to an activity (so the three-minute lesson-beginning rule is maintained), then, twenty minutes later, there is space for some proper, developmental conversation.

Such conversation happens in the lesson transition. I want to argue here that the lesson transitions are key learning moments and need to be planned at least as carefully as the pupils' tasks. If activities are the bricks of the lesson, transitions are the mortar; and, without the mortar, the wall falls down. In this sense, the fourth lesson shape – Shape D (Figure 3.4), with its planned and regular transitions – is the most productive.

What happens in an effective transition? The learning is brought to a head. The activity defines itself for the first time. Time is spent looking back and confirming what's been achieved. Meanings are carefully explained. The earlier learning is checked and evaluated, so that teacher and pupils are confident to move on. The learning objectives become explicit. The next activity is explained in terms of the previous one – the connection between the activities is clear. This is a great deal more than task setting. Often, though, teachers will simply close down one activity and set up the next.

The transition is a rich, concentrated learning source and needs full planning. It sits within the lesson story. You should always know the story of your lesson and you should be able to express it to yourself (and possibly to your students) in a few sentences. Like

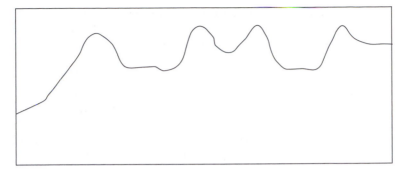

Figure 3.4 Lesson Shape D: multiple transitions.

any story, it depends not upon events but on the links between them. *Having done A, we now understand B. We can now take B and deploy it further, into C.* If you can't see this straightforward narrative in your head before the lesson, you need to pause and consider what those activities have to do with each other. *It's the connections that count.*

I watched an experienced teacher running the simile lesson which I outlined earlier. The children created a boardful of similes, then the time came to gather this learning together, define it, evaluate it and move it on. Verbatim, this is part of what the teacher said at this point.

Teacher (looking with the class at the images on the whiteboard):

> Well, that's quite a character, isn't it? Quite a fascinating character, we should give him a name, should we? What should we call him? And he's got, what's he got? Spots like ten-penny pieces, apparently. Says Laura [Laughter]. And what's this, hair like grass. Which are, as we are saying, this way of saying it's like something, it gives you a picture, we're saying, it makes you laugh. Ears like toadstools, apparently [Laughter]. We're saying they're called similes, because one thing is similar to the other, when we say it's like something, OK, we're calling that expression a simile. Ears like toadstools is a simile. And the spelling. Say simile, but spell siMILE. SimILE, like MILE. It makes it what, more ... [Pupil: Funny]. Yes, more funny. And perhaps more vivid. A picture in the writing.

> And now we're going to have a look at another character,
> and you'll see he has some similes too. Look for his ears. Not
> toadstools. Also his teeth. He's called Timothy. [Distributes
> poem]

In transcript this may appear laboured, even patronising, but the
teacher has recognised that this transition moment is a key
moment where the learning becomes explicit, where the objective
rises to the surface for focused discussion, and where the next
activity is deliberately connected to the last one. Children can see
what is being carried across. The throughline, based on the objective, is revealed.

We have talked here of the lesson as a story; a simple narrative
of connected events which could be summarised in three or four
sentences. There are other helpful metaphors for the lesson.
Perhaps the most helpful is the *lesson journey*. The destination is
the start of journey-planning, just as the learning objective is the
beginning of the lesson plan. Each part of the journey connects
logically to the next part. Children need to be clear about those
connections.

This simple expedient of moving explicit teaching from the
lesson opening to key subsequent transitions (Shape C, or Shape
D) creates a need-to-learn lesson template. Lack of *motivation* is a
key reason for off-task behaviour and this is one way of addressing that. The word itself, of course, means *movement*, and is
related to *momentum*. Inexperienced teachers are often lectured
about 'pace'. Experienced teachers are sometimes accused (by children) of being 'boring'. Let's consider some other ways of creating
momentum in our lessons.

The lesson beginning is a key period. Lesson mood is made or
broken in the first three minutes. Our planning, therefore, needs to
focus on a strong opening. There's nothing worse, nothing harder
to recover from, than a weak beginning. You walk in, you ask
your killer question, and the class just looks at you. You ask it
again; a note of pleading enters your voice. The silence prospers;
tumbleweed is about to blow listlessly across the room. I've died
this death many times and the sense of apathy, of non-co-
operation, is almost irresistible. Twenty minutes into the lesson
you'll have enough momentum to get you out of a hole, but the
first three minutes are vital and you must *plan certain success into
your lesson opening.*

It's easy to do. Consider this checklist for your first three minutes

Start once, not two or three times. If you have to wait a minute, wait, and start cleanly.

Deal straight away with the whole group, not with individuals who want to talk to you.

They should all be required to work within three minutes. Work here doesn't necessarily mean write, but it means more than listening to you. Mark this moment on your lesson plan – *when does everyone (not just volunteers) have to work?* I have watched lesson after lesson where no one who doesn't want to is required to actually do anything (other than appear to be listening to the teacher) for twenty minutes or more. Of course, this is a serious learning issue, but it is also a management issue. Children with nothing to do will eventually misbehave. This can happen right in the middle of what appears to be a highly interactive starter if the only contributors are actually volunteers.

Work from your powerbase – centre-front.

Plan the foothills. Here's another metaphor – if the lesson is a mountain, the opening is the foothills. Everyone must step onto the foothills and everyone can, because they are seductively gentle and almost flat. You are coaxing an animal out of a cage. For example, begin concrete, not abstract. An opening question like, 'Why do we dream?' is likely to bewilder the class, but, 'What did you dream about last night?' is likely to provoke some answers. Start with concrete, anecdotal questions which relate to the pupils' own experiences. 'What was the last argument in your house about?' will get you started; 'Why do families argue?' may only induce the tumbleweed response. (Could you answer that question out of the blue? *Are you testing your opening questions on a willing friend or lover?*)

It's good to start with speaking and listening (and you should always try to avoid the temptation to use silent writing as a management weapon). But don't just ask a question and expect an answer. Allow a minute or two (literally – time it with your watch) of silent jotting first. Now everyone can speak, because they have written something down; you aren't left dependent on volunteers, and no one can opt out if asked, because you can say, 'Just tell us what you've written down...'.

Task setting: QDO

I was tempted to leave this out. I devised it for my trainee teachers and I found that it transformed the task-setting and on/off-task behaviour in their classrooms. When I meet them, years into their careers, they often tell me that QDO is the thing they still use and so, despite its embarrassing simplicity, here it is.

Always QDO when you set a task. It stands for *Questions*, *Deadline* and *Outcome*.

Q is *questions*. Children need a considerable amount of conceptual and practical information from you before they can begin something. In one day I recorded the following questions asked immediately after task-setting. Each is a perfectly reasonable question and each is quite sufficient to prevent a pupil from getting started.

> Is it in the back of our books?
> Do you mean a real person, or a made-up person?
> How long does it need to be?
> Is it based on the book or is it a new story?
> Does it have to rhyme?
> Is it a sketch map?
> Is it to scale?
> Is it set out like a playscript?
> How do you set out a playscript?
> Should I finish this other work first?
> Is this for coursework?
> Can we work in pairs?
> Which page is that on?

There is an infinity of such questions and failure to answer any one of them can produce off-task behaviour. Many children won't even get started. If you are trying to answer all these questions individually around the room, behaviour will deteriorate universally. You should never invite children to start something without running a short whole-class clearing-up activity, based on everyone together answering such questions. Of course, when asked, children will frequently assert that they do understand, that they don't have any questions, then when you tell them to start, they will put hands up and start asking. This just seems to be a trade-union rule for pupils – never own up to not understanding. So there are better ways of handling Q than by simply asking if there are any questions or whether everyone understands; for example, why not have pupils always discuss a new task in pairs, for thirty seconds, and decide if they have any problems? Then they can raise their hands and ask. This is now a part of the task setting; no one has begun, everyone is listening, problems are being raised and solved for everybody. And then you can say to the class, 'Is there now anything that will stop you working when I stop talking?' Such a routine saves time rather than wasting it.

D reminds you that pupils need to know how long they've got. This allows them to plan the work, obviously; it also provides them with an immediate sense of what you're looking for in terms of depth and detail. And, of course, deadlines are highly motivating. I am working hard now on this manuscript because my deadline is looming. So use your watch a lot in the lesson; deadlines generate creative energy and they aren't restricting. You don't have to keep to them, after all.

O is the part of QDO that is often left out. You check that children have no further questions, you tell them how long they've got; you should also tell them where the work is going. Outcome here doesn't mean learning outcome or objective; it means what will happen next. The outcome from a piece of planning might be a GCSE coursework assignment; the outcome from silent poetry writing might be a class reading; the outcome from group discussion might be a feedback to the whole class. Teachers will almost always plan the outcome, but it's surprising how rarely children are informed about it at the outset. Starting off to discuss global warming may engage you. Starting off to discuss global warming knowing that you've got to reach a conclusion in twenty minutes is more engaging. Starting off to discuss global warming knowing that in twenty minutes you're going to have to share your conclusions with the whole class is even more motivating.

Using the subtext

Using QDO is a straightforward example of being proactive. It creates a purposeful atmosphere. Not only does everyone know what's happening, but the *subtext* of the lesson places you in charge, rather than the pupils. Children don't know what subtext is and they can't see it explicitly (that's why it's called *subtext*); but it matters very much. Compare the two possibilities. You set a task; you don't QDO. They listen, they start to work, then find they don't understand. They start asking questions. Apart from interrupting the lesson momentum, this creates a subtext which is saying, 'You haven't explained this properly. You haven't thought it through. Your planning is inadequate. We are having to make sense of your failure to explain. We're not overly impressed.' The children probably aren't thinking this; but they're almost certainly feeling it.

The other option – inviting the questions, making them your idea rather than theirs – runs the opposite subtext. 'I am in charge of this. I've anticipated that there may be difficulties and encouraged you to raise them. I think of you. I have an idea of how you think. I plan this.' You will notice that the latter subtext, apart from being positive and constructive, differs from the first in ownership. The first subtext was theirs. This second subtext is yours.

In fact, subtext is a powerful way of analysing, evaluating and manipulating the effectiveness of your teaching. It is unspoken, subliminal, but inescapable. Let's consider another example. The class behaved badly during the previous lesson. This time, you are determined not to allow this to happen. Before the lesson begins, you make them stand at their desks and you tell them in no uncertain terms about your disappointment. The text of this is straightforward, but, as is often the case, the subtext runs in the opposite direction. The subtext says:

> Ah, yes. We'd more or less forgotten last lesson, but now she has reminded us. We behaved badly and rather enjoyed it. We got away with it. We upset her enough for her to remember it, but she couldn't do anything about it at the time. We really upset her. We're really powerful here. She's fair game.

Over and over again, we remind pupils to behave badly. We publicly reprimand a series of homework defaulters. The text says, 'Several of you haven't done your homework. This is disgraceful and I will not tolerate it.' However, the subtext is saying, 'He told us to do this. We didn't do it. We have ignored his instructions and made a fool out of him. He's reminding us that he's a teacher we ignore. So that's what we'll do.'

Another common example of the dangerous subtext is teacher nagging. The class is working semi-quietly, the noise levels rise, as they always do, after about three minutes. The teacher says, 'Year-

8! You're doing this *quietly*.' The level drops. After three minutes, it rises again. The teacher is now a little more insistent. 'Year-8! I told you! Work *quietly*!' The process flows on. Every three or four minutes, there's another teacher grumble and each one is a little more tetchy than the last. You could draw a graph of it.

The subtext of this is as wrong as it can be. Indeed, the surface text is pretty damning. Consider the comments we make at these times. 'I told you…'; 'How many times…?'. They need to be assertions of authority when in fact they are admissions of failure. The subtext is:

> I have told you to do something. You aren't doing it. Even though I've repeated the instruction several times, and made it clear that it matters, you still aren't doing it. I can't actually make you do what I want. You're in charge.

In fact, teacher nagging is often an offshoot of *stirring the tea*. You are the spoon in the teacup. If you want to stir the class up, you must move around. At that danger moment of starting up group or pair discussions, when you're wondering if they might just sit there self-consciously not saying anything (a tumbleweed moment), you need to get away from the centre-front, start moving around. The noise will start. But when you need them to quieten down, stop stirring; stand still. I've seen so many teachers stirring the class up by walking around, kneeling, disappearing, while periodically nagging them to be quiet. You can't expect both; you can't stir the tea and expect it to remain stationary.

It's this notion of subtext that makes me suspicious of rewards and sanctions policies. They are, of course, essential and, as we said earlier, they are powerful in depersonalising management issues. But they do have a subtext which becomes clear when they are overused. The frequent giving of rewards soon looks like bribery. The reward becomes a payment for services rendered. 'If you finish this, I'll give you a merit mark...' is a fatal transaction. It may work in the short term; the class may want to go to Alton Towers enough to get their heads down; but subtextually this is handing control to the children. As with any purchase, it will become a matter of choice. They may decide to play ball; they may decide not to. No, thanks; I'm not that bothered about merit marks. I'll just sit here and do nothing; I've been to Alton Towers. Working has been made optional. A merit mark is properly an unexpected reward for a job well done, not a currency for bargaining.

Questioning: true and false

Let's consider further how we talk and listen to pupils, paying attention to the subtext which we're creating. Often, these conversations are based on questions. Teachers rightly love questions. If I write *How tall is Prince Phillip?* you cannot help, momentarily, picturing him and thinking about an answer. Questions are difficult to resist. All teachers know that there are different sorts of questions: open, closed, convergent, divergent, factual, rhetorical, opinion-based and so on; and using a range is a good thing. Children like the security of right answers just as much as they like the freedom of exploration and opinion. What matters most is that *they understand what sort of question is being asked.*

This involves the teacher in being open and straightforward about it. You ask a good question, but do you also say, 'There's no right answer to this question'? More to the point, do you sometimes say, 'This question *does* have a right answer'? Children don't mind, but they like to know. The least motivating process, but one I see frequently, is where the teacher asks closed questions as if they were open ones. She has asked for an opinion about something. For example, she has asked how we might go about solving a mathematical problem. Or she has asked us what kind of mood is created by a piece of music. This is an excellent thing to do – pupil opinion is a vital tool in building corroborative and motivated classrooms and it belongs in every subject. All too often, however, the teacher isn't really interested in the pupils' opinions, even though she has asked for them. She knows the correct answer. She grazes the class as they volunteer their answers. I have heard myself doing this so many times. To pupils who aren't supplying the answer I want, I say, 'Ye-es...?' in a sort of rising diphthong, which anyone can tell actually means, 'Yes, but...?' In fact, it means 'No!'. The children know by now that *they are not being asked for their opinions at all; they are being asked to guess the teacher's opinion.* When someone finally provides the right answer, the excited 'Yes!' that rewards that pupil is fundamentally different to the earlier responses. The teacher's relief is palpable.

I have sat in many lessons watching this process and I watch the reactions of pupils who have offered a perfectly good answer to the question. They have been asked for a relevant opinion and have volunteered one, only to be snubbed. Their expressions at these moments are revealing. The mood is one of subliminal irritation. The subtext is clear: you asked for my opinion but you weren't really interested in it. It was a bogus request. If you don't value my opinion, don't pretend that you do. I'll think twice before I volunteer again.

Valuing and validating pupil responses

In fact, this whole area of listening to pupils is seriously important in building good classroom atmosphere. Consider the child who volunteers any kind of contribution. He is making a genuine and quite possibly a difficult commitment to you. There may be all kinds of peer pressure against putting his hand up. Whether his answer is right or wrong, interesting or dull, his subtext is supportive and positive. *You absolutely must reward this commitment.*

All teachers listen to pupils, but the validating of pupil contributions needs to be explicit. Contributions to discussion are validated when their *content* is addressed. Often, the contribution is rewarded with praise and this is helpful; the teacher says 'Good!' or 'Well done!' and moves on to the next answer. It's better than nothing, but a string of 'goods' punctuating a class discussion doesn't motivate at a high level. What motivates is the teacher actually taking the time (a few seconds, probably, no more) to discuss what the pupil has said. When this happens – the teacher asks a question back to the pupil, clarifying and developing a point in the pupil's argument – not only is the learning being progressed, but the balance of relationship in the room is moving towards genuine conversation. 'Good!' is merely assessive; the teacher remains entirely in charge of knowledge and opinion and so shouldn't be surprised if pupils seem reluctant to join in.

The use of the whiteboard as a repository of pupil ideas – a list of one-word reminders of what pupils have said – is a simple but highly motivating tool. The pupils' ideas are published; they remain powerful for a few minutes, rather than disappearing into thin air; there is a symbolism about their words appearing in the teacher's work space.

The YAVA trap

YAVA stands for *You Ask, Volunteers Answer*. Teachers do this all the time; I did it myself for years. Questions are asked; hands go up, keen volunteers speak; the lesson can feel very lively; the teacher will often think that things went rather well. For a couple of minutes, this is an active thing to do; but it has a very limited life. If you're not volunteering, you know that no one is going to bother you. The keen participants at the front can do the work; all you've got to do is keep quiet and avoid the teacher's eye. Don't you remember doing that at school? I spent two years in chemistry staring at the grain on the desk while my fresh-faced chemistry mates rattled on with Mr Webster about molecules and compounds. Everyone was happy, including me.

This is a major learning issue and, as so often, it's also a management issue. One person opting out is a problem; in the YAVA classroom, typically one-third of the pupils are participating. A majority doing nothing is a management time bomb. So limit your YAVA. Of course you must ask questions; of course you must reward volunteers by taking their answers and engaging with them; but consider the fundamental change in the mood of the room when you ask just one non-volunteer to answer (and remember that previous jotting will help). This isn't only a change for the one person you ask; it's a change for all the non-combatants in the room who suddenly realise that they may be next, so they'd better start thinking and listening. Don't abandon your volunteers, but mix them with non-volunteers always when talking to the whole class.

The centrality of speaking and listening

The points above relate classroom talk to learning management, the creation of a strong collaborative atmosphere, the management of the subtext. Talk, however, is even more significant than that. Every subject classroom should feature talk at its heart. Social constructivism concerns the idea that talk is the tool for building new ideas. Children literally need to translate new ideas into their own language and this is done through conversation. And talk builds interest and involvement. It's also the most direct and efficient way of servicing the requirements of literacy policies. Managing talk effectively needs some thought, and this is covered extensively in Chapter 4.

SFC: status, freedom and control

As we said in Chapter 1, little is more important to adolescents than SFC – status, freedom and control. These are the stereotypical obsessions of young people and they are precisely what we attempt to remove from them when they enter a classroom. It's hardly surprising that things don't always run smoothly. It's hardly surprising that pupils sometimes resent you – because SFC is what you have got as a teacher, in abundance. You've stolen it from them.

We talked earlier of lesson planning as creating a need to learn. Planning is where problems are solved and ethos is created. We also need to plan lessons in which you remain authoritative while servicing pupils' background needs. How do you bring freedom into your classroom and remain in charge?

The provision of *choice* is a good start. Every lesson plan is capable of presenting choices to pupils. Where this doesn't occur naturally as essential to the activities, it's usually easy to add it. There can be choice of content or choice of structure. There can be choice of outcome. A pupil can express his understanding in a range of ways, spoken or written. Of course, pupils may tend towards easy or repetitive choices, but you're a teacher – you guide them. This is all fairly obvious, but are you actually looking at your lesson plans and modifying them to provide choice? It's a straightforward way of importing some SFC within a controlled framework.

There are some occasions where choice can range widely. I remember a Year-10 girl who visited Swansea in her holidays and took some photographs in the park where Dylan Thomas set some of his poetry. She became fascinated by this and brought them back to school, where we were able to set up an extensive piece of work involving research, reading, creativity and analysis. She worked more broadly and more deeply than she had ever done before, because she had chosen the subject matter. Again, this is obvious: but where, in your long-term or medium-term planning, are you allowing your pupils to pursue individual interests and to become experts? Experts have status. You are no longer a remover; you are a conferrer. Individuality is being expressed through the work and doesn't have to resort to bad behaviour to show itself.

Such freedoms improve learning management, but they require structures. Your job is to provide frameworks that allow freedoms. Without banks, there is no river. One of the emphasis shifts here is from content to process. Does a child really need to know about a particular piece of music; or does he need to know how we think and talk about music in general? Either can lead to the other; either may be your prime objective; but the lesson which focuses on the latter process of talking about music – the generic concepts, skills and language – can use diverse music chosen variously by pupils, which is subjected to a common analysis framework created by you. They are likely to be more interested. And, given the comparisons and classroom exchanges made possible by this approach – the spread of musical styles, all nevertheless susceptible to the shared analytical activity – they are going to learn about more than one piece of music. They are going to learn how we talk about music in general and how apparent disparities are actually underpinned by common structures. This is a good maxim for our teaching. We will discuss it further in Chapter 5.

SFC: opinion and prediction

It's a scientific fact that adolescents are made up of roughly equal parts of hormones and opinions. For the moment, we will leave hormones alone; but opinions are a major asset in building a collaborative atmosphere. Pupils who have no interest, energy or motivation still have opinions. As always, if you are creating lesson structures which encourage and build on opinions, you are allowing and channelling SFC.

Where in your subject, your scheme of work, your lesson plan, can pupil opinion exist? Of course, it's tempting to think that it suits some subjects and not others. When responding to a poem, for example, children should be used to beginning from personal response. English, we might argue, is a subject where pupil opinion can and should be encouraged.

Sometimes, however, even English teachers are nervous of this. They turn to other approaches, for example to approaches based on author's intention. Thus we ask *What did Shakespeare want us to think about this play?* rather than *How did this play affect you?* And yet other approaches favour historical context. *If you understand the Elizabethans, you understand Shakespeare.* One of the problems with the UK Secondary Frameworks and QCA criteria is their attempts to objectify the unobjectifiable.

We don't actually know what Shakespeare intended. He's dead; we can't ask him; and, if we look at all the books that have been written to explain his intentions to us, we will see that no one else knows or agrees either. Even if we did know, it might not help. It's quite possible, for example, that *The Merchant of Venice* was written as an attack on Jews. If this were actually true, and of course we don't know for sure, would it help us to appreciate it? Would it help our teaching? Would it explain why people still flock to Stratford to see it performed?

What we do have, when we sit down in a classroom with a text or an idea, is our own responses and opinions. We can be sure of those. Of course, in what we might call an 'arts' subject, opinions may be quite easily factored in. We say what we think about poems, music, paintings. Even in these arty lessons, though, opinion can be quite short-lived. It often exists as the initial recovery from reading, looking or listening – a short bout of subjectivity, before the facts kick in. The Mozart stops and we have a few minutes to say what we feel. We don't have very long, because this brief holiday must quickly give way to the proper and serious business of understanding Mozart, his period and his intentions. Luckily, the teacher knows about those, so our opinions will soon be corrected.

This brief flirtation with personal response is only just better than nothing. Strong teaching stays with it for much longer, because confidence in our own responses is the true beginning of analytical ability. All responses are valid and should be considered. For example, if pupils find the painting boring, or stupid, or comical when it's clearly not intended to be, you should stick with those responses. Often they are the route to genuine understanding.

Difficulty and the *stupid syndrome*

I want to explain what I mean by this with reference to a poem, and I apologise for sticking with English for a moment or two more. In English, as in other subjects, we are often confronted with the *stupid syndrome*. It's what happens when pupils are faced with a difficulty and it has three variations. They don't understand the poem, so either *it's stupid* (It's a stupid poem; why doesn't he just say what he means?) or *I'm stupid* (I'll never understand it) or *the teacher's stupid* (Why do we have to read this stuff?). This is an understandable reaction to difficulty.

Let's consider difficulty for a moment more. No one likes difficulty; but it's essential that we meet it every day. If our lessons weren't difficult, no one would be learning anything. We expect to be challenging our pupils at all levels. So reflecting on our attitude to difficulty is an important part of our planning. We want our pupils to face difficulty with confidence. We might say that we want them to find difficult things easy. What are we actually saying to them about this?

Here is the poem. It could be almost any poem. It's by William Blake.

'The Sick Rose'

O Rose, thou art sick.
The invisible worm,
That flies in the night
In the howling storm:

Has found out thy bed
Of crimson joy:
And his dark secret love
Does thy life destroy.

People find this difficult. In an effective classroom, the difficulty isn't a personal failure, but a shared response. If we acknowledge the difficulty rather than being embarrassed or annoyed by it, we can begin to understand the poem. This is because that understanding will come when we begin to define the difficulty. We are going to see how the poem works thanks to, not despite, the difficulty.

The key question here is, 'Why is this poem difficult?' A classroom discussion quickly defines this. For example, the language isn't difficult. The poem has a simple vocabulary. It has a simple childish structure. In recognising this, we are already making valid analytical statements. The difficulty, of course, is in what the poem is actually about. Is Rose a girl, ill, or perhaps sexually corrupt in her bed of 'crimson joy'? Or is she actually a flower in a flowerbed? In an insecure classroom, where difficulty is a personal failure, pupils will be anxious to get this right. It must be one or the other, but I fear I'm too stupid to know which. In a secure classroom, where personal response is habitually valued, pupils will readily admit that they aren't sure, or that they are vacillating between one reading and the other. We don't know what she is – and this takes us straight to the heart of the poem's energy, because, when we see Rose as both a flower and a girl, the one image superimposed on the other, we realise that the poem tells us about the transience of human beauty. A young girl's beauty is as short-lived as a flower's. Our discussion of difficulty has taken us straight to the heart of the poem. The secure, validating classroom has worked and the anxious one has failed.

What we are saying, then, is that difficulty should be welcomed into our lessons. It should be acknowledged as a token of our learning. It should be discussed as part of our response. One of the best questions a teacher can ask a class is, 'Why do we find this difficult?'. This is a very different question to 'Why do *you* find this difficult?'. In any new piece of learning, in any subject, defining the difficulty can be the precursor to understanding. As ever, this needs to be proactive. Your planning anticipates the problems, because difficulty is an essential and proper feature of the new and challenging learning, not an unfortunate accident. How powerful and reassuring it is to say to a class, before reading the poem, 'I expect you to find this difficult. I did, when I first read it. Let's see; and let's see what's difficult about it.'

This validation of pupil response lends SFC to your classroom. It introduces opinion. Opinion, as we've said, is important to adolescents. Possibly, their world view is that teachers have the facts, while students have the opinions. The classroom balance of fact-

and-opinion usually plays strongly in favour of facts. This is inevitable, but only up to a point. Adjusting towards opinion is engaging for your pupils.

And opinion isn't just the province of arts subjects. I'm often surprised, for example, at how little classroom discussion I see in science or mathematics lessons. Science presents topic after topic in which personal experience and opinion have much to offer. Pupils can discuss pollution, carbon emissions, global warming. They can consider a post-oil world. They can discuss why science seems to be a boys' subject. These activities feature personal response – could *you* live without a car? – as constructivist pathways into concept-based conversations. This is good learning and it's also good, motivating management. Of course, such discussions need planning and structure; this is examined in detail in Chapter 4.

A powerful subset of opinion is prediction. Prediction can feature in almost every lesson. It engages children because it requires personal opinion and because it lays down a comparison pattern. When we've predicted, we want to know if we're right. We become interested in what's going to happen. Halfway through a novel, we predict the ending. In fact, we predict the ending regularly. We become fascinated by the possibilities. We argue with each other about various outcomes. And when the ending is different from our prediction, we compare the two.

When we do this, we are imitating life. In life, we guess and predict all the time. When we're reading a book, we're predicting the ending: we don't need a teacher to tell us to do that. Agatha Christie made a good living out of this impulse. In fact, when we read a paragraph or even a sentence, we are predicting the ending. Our eye isn't travelling linearly, it's darting around. When we go shopping, we predict how busy the town is likely to be and where we'll be able to park. Prediction is how we make sense of the world.

Consider, then, how you can structure prediction into your subject teaching. In science, we can guess at how an experiment might be constructed to make a particular discovery. We can guess how surrounding a beaker with felt will affect its warming. Our guesses may be wrong; when we understand why, we are learning about scientific process. Hypothesis and prediction are essential scientific concepts. In history, we can predict outcomes from sets of circumstances and then find out whether we were right. In music, we can predict how a symphony might end (which of the earlier themes will be taken up? Will it be a big, noisy ending or a quiet, peaceful one?). When we do this, we aren't just playing a game. To back the right horse, you have to study the form. Prediction work forces close analytical engagement with given ideas.

One issue with the UK strategies and frameworks is the erosion of creativity. This is now widely recognised. It is true of teachers' planning and children's learning. One of the saddest remarks I ever heard was from the head teacher of a primary school being interviewed in the early days of the literacy strategy. 'Oh, yes,' she said, talking of quite young children. 'They all know what onomatopoeia is. But they haven't sung a song for six months.' Indeed, this theme resurfaces against various recent initiatives. The Hargreaves report on changes to the post-16 curriculum regretted the encroachment of the new specifications on enrichment activities (sport, drama, music) in the sixth form. More recently, bodies such as Ofsted have noticed and commented on the lack of creativity in our classrooms. We peer at such reports over the piles of strategies and league tables which separate us from them and from common sense.

Creativity belongs in all subjects, not just 'creative' ones. It is greatly valued by business leaders and politicians, as well as artists. It is synonymous with intellectual versatility and agility. Problem solving, prediction and personal response are all aspects of creativity. Business Studies pupils can design and market new products. They can talk about their own part-time jobs when discussing issues of workforce motivation. PE students create dance routines and new sports, with new rules. They predict the outcome of a particular approach to playing a sport. Science pupils predict as a precursor to any investigation. MFL pupils use role play and prediction in stories. Developing such approaches broadens the teaching base and offers a differentiated curriculum. It also introduces SFC into your classroom; the pupils have a voice. It strengthens learning. You don't learn to drive by watching the driver; you learn by sitting in the driving seat.

Ownership

I was watching the end of a history lesson. A difficult Year-10 class and an experienced teacher. She was working hard and the pupils were trying, in both senses of the word. We came to the plenary; a routine clearly well recognised by everybody. She wrote *Got* and *Not Got* on the whiteboard, and the pupils were extremely vocal in telling her what they'd understood from the lesson and, even more emphatically, what they hadn't. The list of *Not Gots* was then examined. There was some peer teaching then; pupils who *had* got it were explaining, mostly at a yell, to those who hadn't. She let this go on for a couple of minutes, and then a few *Not Gots* were removed from the list. In fact, they became *Gots*. The students watched as their achievement list grew a little and their problem list shrank. These were a highly energetic few moments, pupils spurred along by the desire to affect the lists and to explain things to each other. This was not a quiet, reflective plenary – it had the atmosphere of a street market or a football match – but it was extraordinarily exciting.

After a couple of minutes, the exchanges were brought to a close. A great deal had been achieved. Some pupils knew more than they had before. Some pupils had become teaching experts and had rehearsed their own understanding of the lesson ideas. But even more to the point, the whole class had participated in joint learning. The business was to get this stuff learned. The teacher had led the lesson, but this plenary had been a joint exercise. The learning was a shared activity. A passing Deputy Head may have suspected a riot, but this was expert teaching. Adolescent energy was deployed by the simple structure of *Got, Not Got* and the unquestioned underlying assumption that learning had to be done.

Ownership, like *proactivity*, is a maligned piece of jargon. It is far from meaningless. If you own something, you don't want to break it. There are many routines that can strengthen the sense of pupils owning their own learning.

The plenary described above had more to come. The teacher looked at the *Not Gots* and discussed with the class what to do tomorrow. Which of the items needed teaching again? Why hadn't they understood them? What could she do to make it easier?

Consider the power of questions like these: plenary questions where a main plenary function – evaluation for future planning – is carried out not at home alone at the end of the day, but there and then with the children. This is powerful with any age or ability group. It is a learning activity in itself. What do we need to do tomorrow? How might we do it? These are the best kinds of predictions. They absolutely invoke SFC. They effectively evaluate the closing lesson. They place the learning somewhere between teacher and pupils as something to be considered and fostered jointly.

These processes can run throughout the lesson. I remember teaching speech marks to a Year-8 mixed-ability class. Their understanding of speech marks was all over the place. In fact, speech marks are quite difficult (though not as difficult as the apostrophe which, thank heavens, is currently on the critical list). Do you know exactly when and where you use a capital letter inside speech marks? Many English graduates certainly don't. I do, but that's only because I'm much older than they are.

I explained to the class that, in their stories, they were misusing speech marks in various ways. I was preparing to explain the rules to them and, when they realised this, they groaned audibly. Not only is it boring to listen to the rules, but (more to the point) we know we probably won't remember them or apply them in a week's time. I paused. 'Well,' I said. It was a genuine question. 'I know the rules, and you don't. What are we going to do?'

The objective is non-negotiable. We can't opt out of speech marks. But the learning process may sometimes be up for discussion. In fact, I put my Year-8s into small groups and asked them to come up with their ways of finding out about speech marks. After an extremely engaged discussion, they offered a range of suggestions, which included:

- I could go ahead and tell them the rules, and they would then have to use them six times in the next week, to help them remember;
- they could research the rules in English text books;
- they could ask their parents;
- they could ask older children, who might know;
- they could write to the local newspaper who, they believed, should know;
- they could look at conversations in the class reader (a novel we were reading together) and work out the rules from there.

This was a mixed bunch of suggestions; we tried more than one of them. The editor of the local paper sent us some helpful comments on punctuation, some of which were wrong; and older children and parents didn't seem to be much help. From all this, we concluded that speech marks were pretty problematic things and we weren't stupid for not understanding them. But the final idea in this list – investigating expert sources, deducing the rules from correct usages – struck me as an excellent idea. That is how we learned speech marks. They looked at a passage from the novel, which I chose quite carefully, and they answered key questions (such as, 'Where do you put the capital letter?'). Weeks later they still remembered. This was active learning, of course; but what was most exciting and effective was that the activities had been conceived and devised by them. Consider your planning. Where are you allowing this level of input, this degree of sharing in the learning? Just as planning is the most important thing a teacher does, so collaborative planning is the most powerful kind of collaboration.

Of course, this kind of flexibility demands high-order skills from the teacher. There are ways of narrowing the range, making it more realistic while still maintaining a sense of shared endeavour. Offering pupils a choice of three possible ways of learning something, listed by you, invites engagement and discussion. They reject two ways and choose the third, but for each, they have to offer their reasons. Or they can design the plenary. Plenaries, it

has to be said, can be fairly deadly. We return to the learning objectives and solemnly assert that we've met them. After all, we can't go to break until we do. This means almost nothing, and, indeed, plenaries in general are a pretty undeveloped and ineffectual part of our teaching. Starters have been debated and honed, but plenaries are often brief afterthoughts. The plenary is the main evaluator, and evaluation is crucial to developing both teaching and learning (see Chapter 7). Why not allow pupils to plan the plenary? Say to them, in effect, 'You know what the learning objective was. You know what we've done to try to learn it. We've got ten minutes to check whether we've learned it or not. How can we check that?' The very act of designing the plenary (perhaps in pairs and then whole-class discussion) carries the consolidatory and evaluative functions of the plenary itself. If they can design a plenary, they've probably understood the lesson. It's collaborative and creative, it offers SFC and motivation. This is how we want our teaching to be.

Chapter 4

Literacy

Do not skip this chapter

You might be tempted to ignore this. Cross-curricular themes don't have a great history. You're teaching Renaissance painting and someone asks you where the numeracy is. Or the citizenship in congruent triangles. People are constantly waving audits at you, one agenda flying past after another; it's not surprising if you just want to be left alone to get on with it.

Literacy strategies are particularly insistent. They began a long time ago, and the Bullock Report reinvented them in 1975, to be followed by the fabulously well resourced National Literacy Strategy. I'm not arguing the case for all of these initiatives here, though I don't doubt the value of many of them, and (by the way) the principle of cross-curricularity is long overdue for revival in secondary teaching. Hiving everything off into subjects is one of the cruel and restrictive practices we arbitrarily force upon children when they become eleven years old. These are important issues; but what I'm arguing here (perhaps controversially) is that literacy isn't like the other strategies. It's fundamental to our teaching, in a way that even numeracy, important though it is, cannot be. We teach almost everything through the medium of spoken and written language. Literacy isn't an add-on. It isn't really a 'strategy'. It's our principle tool, and to be brilliant teachers we have to be constantly alive to its demands and its potential.

Some theory: an aside

I hope that this book is more practical than theoretical. Nothing happens in a classroom, however, that doesn't concern learning theory and it's timely now to glance at some theory which places language at the heart of teaching.

Vygotsky's work – an aspect of *social constructivist theory* – concerns what he called the 'zone of proximal development'. This 'zone' stands between the pupil's current learning and the next level. Any teacher must be thinking about how the 'zone' is to be crossed; how the learner is to move on. A central answer for Vygotsky involves language, especially talk. You literally translate new ideas into your own language, using your own examples. For example, as you read this, you might be thinking of an instance of coming across a new idea and restating it to yourself in your own words so that you understood it. In remembering that example, you are actually applying the process to the ideas in this paragraph. When you say,

> Oh yes, that's like when I had to talk to Paul about the difference between a spreadsheet and a table, and he said, Well, a spreadsheet is really a mathematical thing, and a table is a formatting thing, and I said, Oh, you mean a table is more presentational, but a spreadsheet does calculations and things...

you are actually translating this paragraph into your own language. When you spoke to Paul about spreadsheets, you were doing the same thing.

In practical terms, this aspect of Vygotsky places talk in a central position and this has direct implications for your lesson planning. Where is the talk and how is it structured? At a very basic level, I never set a task for students without asking them to discuss the task in pairs and then to raise queries about it (QDO). This routine adds about ninety seconds to your task-setting but saves much time, misunderstanding and wasted energy. Try it, and eavesdrop. And think about when a colleague asks you to do something. Don't you immediately need to say to the person next to you, 'What does he mean? Does he mean like this...? Is he talking about...?' and so on. Let the children restate the task in conversation with each other. Let them re-explain key concepts, redefining them in their own terms. The power of simple pair work is enormous and in using it you are showing your understanding of social constructivism.

Bruner offers specific thoughts about the conversations that might happen between pupil and teacher. The teacher offers *scaffolding* to prompt and support the learner through a curriculum which grows through stages of complexity as the learning matures. The teacher adjusts her talk with pupils by (for example) asking questions and making spontaneous interventions to point children in the right direction, and these exchanges diminish as the learning becomes more assured.

It's a helpful metaphor; the scaffolding is essential but temporary, allowing the building of the learning to get off to a safe and confident start. For example, the teacher may offer a writing frame which provides a fairly prescriptive format for a history essay. Such a frame may be based on the topics and first sentences of a sequence of paragraphs. It means that everybody can get started and that most people's worries about how to structure the essay are reduced. They know what order to put the paragraphs in, how each paragraph should start, how they should talk about historical evidence and where their conclusion should be. But the scaffolding may not end there. The teacher should also be running individual and group-based conversations which allow him to offer prompting questions and suggestions around the room; the scaffolding moves from whole-class, formally structured scaffolding to semi-spontaneous, individual support. Certainly a formal scaffold like a writing frame has limitations – it can restrict creativity and originality – and the teacher's individual conversations may need to compensate for this. At some point, like stabilisers, the scaffold will be removed.

So you should consider where and how you need to scaffold. There are several recognised stages of scaffolding. The current UK Secondary Strategy – including the National Literacy Strategy – favours scaffolding; so there is a useful example of how an aspect of social constructivist learning theory has been taken up in curricular policies and enacted in schools.

Of course, it's just common sense that pupils need particular help in getting started. Beginnings are very important in teaching. Do your lesson plans show your scaffolding methods? They might include writing frames, examples, sets of written instructions, prompt scripts, shared or guided writing, models and demonstrations. In one day a pupil may be asked to write three *essays* (or assignments or sets of notes or reviews) and each one of the three, set by a different teacher in a different lesson, will have different requirements. A history assignment in the morning looks and sounds fundamentally different to an English assignment in the afternoon. Schools work very hard to reduce such confusions, but there will always be a range of definitions and variation of requirements. One thing that you can and must do is define what you mean, for example, by 'assignment'. That is as much a part of the learning as the subject matter of the essay itself. This defining process is often best delivered through scaffolding.

Teacher language

Let's continue by considering your own language as a teacher. Your voice is your main teaching aid. You can actually, consciously use its pitch, tone and pace to underpin the shape and changes of the lesson. Do you drop and slow your voice when moving from a lively passage to a quiet one?

As we've said, the lesson has its story. This is what your plan is based on. We will do A; this will enable us to understand something (we'll call it B). B will be defined in a transition and then carried forward into the next activity, C. It's the carrying forward that counts. There is a thread, not a series of separate activities. If you have a clear and simple story, you have a coherent lesson. Obviously, then, pupils are most likely to make sense of the lesson if they understand the story, too.

There's nothing childish or twee about this idea of lesson story. We may at times think that our Western, modernist culture has abandoned narrative, has relegated story-time to the nursery. Nothing could be further from the truth. Culturally, we are besotted by stories. We are obsessed with television soaps and crime dramas. We perceive politics and world events in terms of stories. We make up stories about real people ('celebrities') to make them available to us. This last is a key thought. A famous footballer and his tuneless wife become accessible to us because of the stories which are created about them.

So the lesson story is crucial to accessibility. It lives in the planning of coherent and connected activities, as we've said; it can also live in teacher language. I don't mean that you should be using the phrase 'lesson story' with pupils (although you might: what about 'Tell me the lesson story in three sentences' as a plenary?). A plot is a series of connected events; the lesson becomes a story *when the connections are clear*. There's no reason why you shouldn't be explicit about the story from start to finish. You sketch out the whole story at the beginning. 'We will do this, and then, having established that, we will do this other thing...' The route map – a sketch map – is laid out before them in words, and perhaps literally, in a whiteboard diagram. And then at each key transition moment, the lesson stage is explicitly announced. 'We are now moving into a period of quiet. We've had some animated discussion, but the next stage is where we need to reflect and jot some personal thoughts...' This is more than instruction or task-setting; it's more than the (sometimes deadly) writing of the lesson objectives on the whiteboard; it's a recurring and explicit reminder of where we are, what stages and moods we're leaving and entering. 'We said that we'd pause at this point to gather those thoughts. That's where we are now. We've reached that point...' The lesson moment is given explicit identity and value within the overall lesson shape. Don't just talk about the learning; talk about the lesson.

This is not the only way in which your own language generates a constructivist atmosphere. Teacher-talk is vital and is often at its best when most explicit. We've already talked about questioning and the need not only to plan a range of questions but to be explicit and straightforward about your own questions. It's good to say, 'There's no right answer to this question...', or to say, 'This question *does* have a right answer.' Or you could ask the pupils: 'Do you think my question is the kind that only has one answer?'. When pupils start discussing the language of the lesson, as well as its facts and ideas, they are involved in meta-learning. They are thinking at a high level.

But teacher-talk is more than questioning. Teachers shouldn't talk for too long, of course; but they shouldn't be afraid of teaching. They should be authoritative in subject knowledge as well as learning management. How are you explaining things to pupils?

Differentiation (see Chapter 6) can be achieved by teacher language. When you know what your key moments are – the golden moments of explicit explanation, the confirmation of ideas, the rich transition content – how are you using language to present a range of access to your thoughts? You can plan two or three ways of describing these key points, but can we be more systematic than that? For example, are you using figurative language?

Figurative language is imagery – similes, metaphors. Please keep reading; this isn't a section for English teachers. A simile is a comparison, and poets and politicians – who are, like teachers, professional communicators – love them because they make accessible the inaccessible. That is precisely what teaching does. So here is a language technique which is designed to do exactly what teachers need.

As a poet, I write: 'His skin was as disrupted and pale as screwed-up newspaper.' I don't do this to show off, or to make my writing (as children insist on believing) more difficult, or even more interesting. I do it because you, my reader, haven't seen his skin. You can't have, because I just made him up. But you *have* seen screwed-up newspaper. That is what imagery does. It translates the unknown into the known by a process of comparison.

An equation is a pair of scales, perfectly in balance. We may not have the same things in each scale, but they add up to the same, and if we change one side, we have to change the other, or it will collapse. No maths teacher ever said that to me; it took me a few months to work it out for myself (because I .was good at English, not maths). When I did see that metaphor, it genuinely helped me with the maths of equations. A good teacher would have those images ready as part of her planned explanations. A brilliant teacher might go so far as to invite pupils to create their own images. I could have told her about my scales. I wonder how she would have reacted.

Another broadening technique for teacher-talk is the use of examples and anecdotes. Exemplification is crucial to learning, because, like similes and metaphors, it's a translation strategy. You are, in history, dealing with the First World War and you want to explain that this is a war of *attrition*. This is warfare that proceeds by constant harassment and weakening of the enemy; and that's a definition. You may explain to pupils that that's what it is; but, as we've said, defining isn't learning. We don't extend our vocabulary by reading dictionaries. One problem with such a

definition is that, to a child who is not a professional soldier or military tactician, this seems to define *all* wars. Surely all armies try to harass and weaken the enemy? Which armies seek to comfort and strengthen the enemy? What's your point?

In Chapter 2, we considered two stick men. One stick man on his own tells us nothing, but when we have two, we begin to see distinctions. This is significant in our development as thinking human beings. Babies don't know where they end and their mothers begin. As they grow, they learn distinctions and differences. By the time they are adolescents, they are quite certain of the boundaries between them and their parents. So one way of defining learning is by this growing ability to see differences, to compare and contrast. To support this growth and to exploit it, our lessons need to be packed with comparison opportunities. You may only be teaching attrition warfare, but you need other kinds of warfare in your lesson so that attrition may be sharply understood against its alternatives.

Now, this may look like a tall order. It's a cumbersome business, finding other kinds of war just for comparison purposes, dragging in wars we aren't even studying. Hours of planning and teaching may be wasted here, just to define a word. I've got more and better things to do.

First of all, we need to return to the ideas of learning objectives and the lesson shapes we outlined in Chapter 3. The flat-line lesson just proceeds and teaches as it finds. *Attrition* comes up at some point. It's explained and defined. We move onto the next thing. Pupils have notes. We're getting on with it. In fact, we're getting *through* it. This may feel productive, but the chronological generation of notes on various related topics as they occur offers no learning focus, differentiation or rich value to anything. We are in danger of working for our own sense of well-being, rather than for lasting pupil achievement. Teach twelve things in a lesson and pupils are quite likely to forget eight and confuse the other four. This is the pebble-dash approach to teaching. It has helped me to fail a number of examinations, though I had book-loads of notes. It's quite brave to turn away from this and to actually focus on learning. If you teach two or three things well, they have a chance of making sense, and sticking.

It's still asking a lot to expect you to produce a whole range of different historical wars for the pupils to compare just so that they get *attrition*. This is where exemplification comes in. Much closer to home – in fact much closer to the pupils themselves – are all the examples you need. There's another kind of war that is quick, sharp and defined. It has clear objectives and doesn't last very long. This is the opposite of *attrition*. Even just saying that is better than nothing. We already have the beginning of a sense of what you're talking about. So it may be a teaching rule that no new idea is introduced by definition alone. At least, the definition is set against others with which it compares.

Children don't know much about wars, but they know plenty about arguments. This is constructivism again. It's also just plain, efficient common-sense practice. Start with what they know. Have them talking in pairs about different types of argument they've had. Were they over with quickly? Did they kiss and make up? Or did the argument go on for months, becoming a drawn-out grudge, getting more and more bitter? Becoming, in fact, an argument of attrition. They can see the difference. They didn't know there were names for this sort of thing.

Now we have a lesson which matches Shape C in our need-to-learn process (Chapter 3). We are not just spending a couple of minutes on attrition as it comes up (Shape A). We aren't beginning by defining *attrition* and then applying it to the First World War (Shape B). We are creating a need to learn by contriving starter activities which explore the concepts of different types of warfare *before* approaching the language.

How do you run such a lesson? Speaking and listening is where literacy lives, much more than in those tedious 'literacy policies' which tell us all exactly how to correct a spelling mistake. Pair work is a major asset here, and every subject should be doing it. It's a safe place for pupils to try out new ideas and get them quickly peer-reviewed without public exposure. In pairs or small groups, they need key questions, not just topics, for discussion. One advantage of the Shape C lesson is that the work can begin at the level of the informal, personal and concrete. This must be reflected in your opening questions. 'Are there different sorts of arguments?' is the question you want answered, but it's not the question to start with. Test your questions on somebody before the lesson. They need to be easy to answer; the conversation has to get started. 'Why do we argue?' is even more abstract, almost philosophical; it's also pretty much unanswerable. 'What was the last argument you had?' is the question you're looking for. It's personal, concrete and anecdotal – which is precisely why children find it interesting to talk about. Give them some key questions, let them discuss in pairs or small groups, then begin a whole-class explanation of arguments. They are, in fact, experts on different argumentative tactics. They will tell you. And on the basis of their anecdotes they will start to see patterns of warfare and the lesson will move towards the more abstract and the more formal.

And so you reach a transition point where, finally, *attrition* is defined, spelled and examined. We are then ready to move into the First World War. This has taken a long time and some teachers will grumble that they haven't got time for this sort of thing; they've got a war to fight. By which approach are youngsters in with a chance of remembering all this in three months' time?

Managing discussion

Group discussion is vital area to literacy and learning. Ideas can be practised and structured. Consider, for example, the notion of *oral drafting*. Children can prepare for a piece of formal writing by discussion as well as through written notes. Of course, they can rehearse, trial and review their ideas in conversation much more efficiently and quickly than they could ever do in writing. They can also quickly understand key features of discursive writing from their discussion work. For example, they can understand the need to provide evidence for personal opinions. In a written essay they will often simply assert their views, but in conversation they will be challenged by others and forced to explain and support their statements. With your explicit linking, this can be transferred into written form. From their discussion work, pupils now see why evidence is a necessary part of mounting an argument.

Similarly, in (say) a discursive essay on global warming, you want children to recognise and refute arguments against their own viewpoints. You want them to say:

> Of course, some people argue that there's no such thing as man-made climate change. There is a view that, if we are in a period of warming, this is part of a natural cycle, and we can't do anything about it. However, there are now growing statistics against these arguments, and I believe that...

Citing and refuting counter-arguments is a sophisticated feature of discursive writing and it's best approached through discussion work, where those opposing views will naturally occur and be argued with. Once again, your linking of the discussion to the writing will enrich the final written product.

In fact, a discursive essay, in any subject, resembles a debate or a trial. The formal debate, or the staged trial (oil companies charged with climate change; homework research for defence and prosecution) exactly mirrors the balanced structure of a good discursive essay, with its for-and-against shape, its supporting evidence, its final conclusion.

In the UK, the *Every Child Matters* agenda requires us to consider children's health and safety, their enjoyment and achievement, and their economic well-being. Much of this activity happens beyond the classroom; in fact, it's becoming conventional to regard the *enjoy-and-achieve* strand as the main focus for a secondary subject teacher. Of course, group discussion supports *enjoy-and-achieve*. *Economic well-being*, however, seems less easy to place in some classrooms. How do art or RE contribute to economic well-being? They can, easily. Economic well-being stems, in part, from the ability to function in a workplace – to be able to communicate, listen, articulate, negotiate, argue, assert, give way, co-operate, synthesise. These are key work skills and they are fostered in every classroom that runs group discussions. It doesn't even matter what the discussions are about; they are learning to work together.

However, you can't just put people into groups and give them a topic. Speaking and listening may be unpopular because it's perceived as being difficult to manage. In fact, it's a management ally; it releases all kinds of classroom pressures; but, like everything else in teaching, it needs prepared structures. In fact, it's an extremely disciplined set of activities. Good drama lessons are highly disciplined. Sport, where children wear odd clothes and charge about aggressively and competitively, is subject to the most complex of rule systems. Discipline and activity are mutually dependent and mutually supportive.

Let's consider, for example, the management of group discussion. What are the management danger points? Children may not talk; some may dominate to the detriment of others in the group; they may talk about *Eastenders*; they may make too much noise; you may not be able to properly monitor or control the discussion. Setting aside the point that any good teacher takes risks from time to time, we can easily deal with these danger points by good planning.

Are you thinking about the formation of the group?

Four people is enough. Larger groups split or isolate individuals. Varying grouping is essential – friendship groups, mixed-gender groups, extrovert/introvert mixes, random groups where you just meet someone new to work with.

Are you helping with the internal working of the group?

Groups are so often given a topic and left to it. Here as ever you have to plan from the pupils' viewpoint. Will they be able simply to get on with it? Do you need to advise them how to proceed? Do they need to define their group roles, such as group leader, group note-maker, group arguer?

This last is a brilliant addition to group work. One member is appointed devil's advocate (though you might not use the phrase). His job is to listen to the arguments and counter them. This is fun but also creates a whole new dynamic in the discussions. You can create other generic roles as well – such as a group pacifier, a group problem-solver. It is worth taking time over the definition of these roles. For example, the group note-maker is more than just a dogsbody; it is her job to pause the discussion from time to time to recap and agree on the positions reached so far. The leader does more than simply keeping it going; for example, she must ensure that everybody speaks and is heard. Brilliant teachers spend time on these roles, preferably by creating role cards for all members of the group which define their responsibilities. Even members with no additional job have a role card which defines the whole business of offering views, offering evidence, listening to counter-arguments, considering how to respond, moving towards compromise, and so on.

It may take you an hour to make a set of group-discussion role

Table 4.1 **Discussion group roles**

Leader	Ensure that everyone gets a turn.
	Ensure that everyone listens.
	Ensure that the discussion brief is covered.
	Watch the time.
Note-maker	Record the discussion.
	Pause the discussion from time to time and summarise it with the group, checking your understanding.
	Contribute to feedback.
Arguer	Listen to and challenge arguments and opinions.
	Ask others to justify their arguments.
	Offer counter-arguments, especially if the discussion is quiet.
Pacifier	Help leader and members to reconcile opposing views.
	Offer compromises.
	Discuss changes of view among members.
Member	Offer views and evidence for them.
	Listen to other views, possibly making notes.
	Modify your views if appropriate.
Feedback organiser	Work with leader, note-maker and all group members to organise feedback.
	Check feedback requirements.
	Keep appropriate notes.
	Remind leader and group of timing so that feedback can be addressed.

cards like this, but you can use them over and over again and your pupils will become used to them and need them less and less.

Are they preparing for the discussion?

They can prepare by making relevant notes which they bring to the discussion so they all have a flying start. Think about useful structures for this. A simple continuum – a line with *totally in favour of fox-hunting* at one end and *totally against fox-hunting* at the other, with a mid-point ready marked – will allow pupils to focus on where they stand. They put their personal marks on the line and write a few sentences explaining their decision; they arrive at the group discussion with this information already in place.

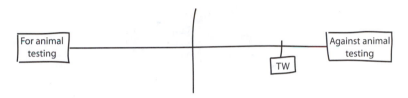

Figure 4.1 Continuum line.

Are you structuring the discussion?

Pupils need clear structure. You need to break down the discussion into timed components such as ten minutes for opening comments, time for main discussion, and so on. But you also need to structure the content. The discussion may focus on a prompt sheet. The prompt sheet might be:

- a series of questions to answer;
- a series of statements to place in order of preference;
- a series of statements to sort into given columns;
- a series of continua (see above) for group agreement and completion;
- a series of statements (or a single statement) with which to agree or disagree;

and so on.

Do you QDO?

They need to know how long they've got, and they need frequent reminders. They need warning as they approach the end. In particular, they need advance warning of the nature of any feedback. Preparing the feedback to the whole class is a task in itself and they need help with doing this, including a time allocation for it. They can't have a lively discussion and then just cobble together a feedback at the last minute. They need help with its content; they need to think about purpose and audience; they need to practise it.

Are you monitoring the groups?

You will develop a sense of when groups are flagging and need your subtle and brief intervention. It's easy to tell whether a group has strayed off the point and often all you need to do is to go and stand near it. You need to combine your accessibility to the groups with your visibility to the whole class. Often, teachers set pupils off on activities and then plunge into the body of the room, kneeling at tables (which is a good thing) while the behaviour in the room drops as the noise levels rise. This can go on for twenty minutes and things get steadily worse because the teacher has effectively, almost literally, disappeared. Children need periodic sight of you to remember where they are and what the background structures are. Don't circle from group to group – for one thing, this makes your path predictable. Visit a group, then return to the centre-front and stay there; you don't have to speak, or do teacher-glaring, just be visible; then visit another group.

Of course, pupils will digress; they will talk about football and boyfriends, you have to accept this, just as you have to accept that their minds will wander when they're sitting in silence. Of course, when they're talking, at least you know what they're talking about!

The point about all of this is that speaking and listening is a central part of your teaching. Discussion work isn't a holiday from the real thing; it's at the heart of it and so it needs planning attention and careful management. Schools whose literacy policies are based largely on writing, and are (sometimes) in danger of deteriorating into neglected marking policies, would do much better to transform their literacy policies into vibrant cross-curricular approaches to speaking-and-listening.

I want to conclude and underline this discussion by comparing two lessons that I watched on the same day. They are English lessons, but, more to the point, they should both be literacy lessons. One succeeds because it weaves its teaching language around a clear objective; and one takes a flat-line, *learn-as-we-go* approach.

The two lessons provided a telling illustration of the need to plan to objectives which are few and small. The more local and specific the objective, the better. In the first lesson, the teacher did a poem. 'Doing' a text consists of working through it, giving notes, having discussions, trying to make it interesting as you go along. I taught like this for many years. This is a Shape A lesson. The poem on this occasion was by Wilfred Owen and the teacher and pupils worked manfully through it. After about half an hour, they had notes on the First World War, Owen, the sonnet form, alliteration, onomatopoeia, rhyme and rhythm, the meanings of various new words in the poem, symbolism, metaphor, assonance, bathos and irony. These things had cropped up as they went along and the teacher had made a reasonable job of explaining them.

The chances of the children remembering all or most of this

learning and being able to reapply it in the future are slim. Almost any one of these concepts is worthy of being properly taught, from the context of the poem, using other examples, using creativity and analysis. A lesson which began from the notion that Owen's poetry makes telling use of onomatopoeia (for example) would build towards an understanding of the term through consideration of onomatopoeia in jokes, newspaper headlines, other poems and the pupils' own creative writing. It would compare onomatopoeic writing with non-onomatopoeic equivalencies to appreciate its effects. It would take time to present multiple approaches to the understanding. It would build in a Shape C way from playing with the sounds of words to a definition of the central term. And it would not limit the pupils' responses to the poem as a whole, because onomatopoeia would be discussed in terms of its effects on the reader, its contribution to the emotional vividness of Owen's language.

But the teacher didn't do this. She taught a wide range of things which were connected only by having to do with the one poem. Whether the pupils roundly understood these concepts was another matter, as is whether they remembered them a fortnight later.

On the same day I watched a lesson on Act 3, Scene 5 of *Romeo and Juliet*. The scene features *ambiguity*. Juliet is talking to her mother about her forbidden love for Romeo, but her mother thinks she's talking about her grief over the death of her cousin Tybalt. Juliet deliberately hides behind this misunderstanding. She wants to express her grief, but of course she mustn't own up to her relationship with the forbidden Romeo. She isn't lying to her mother, but she isn't telling the truth, either.

The teacher had decided not to 'do' the scene but to *build the whole lesson around the single objective that pupils would understand its ambiguity*. In fact, it is two objectives: to understand the concept of ambiguity, and then to see it in the conversation between the Capulet women. What looks at first sight like a single objective is often in fact several: the concept must be understood, and then its use in the given context must be appreciated; these activities are not identical. Of course the text provides the context for the generic understanding, but your planning has to take account of this complexity and take pupils stage-by-stage to real understanding. In this case, the teacher had decided that, if the pupils could leave the room understanding ambiguity and its power in this scene, able to explain it to their mums at home and to remember it in three days' time, then that would be an hour well spent.

From one single idea, the teacher constructed a lesson which began with a discussion of a scene from *Home and Away* in which deliberate ambiguity featured, followed by a paired role play in which pupil A (teenager) had to convince pupil B (parent) that she wasn't going to a party at her friend's house, even though she was. She had to do this without lying, under some quite fierce questioning (*Will there be lots of people there? Well, a few of my friends...*). So, at the key transition points between such activities, the notion of ambiguity becomes explicit and roundly understood, and the pupils recognise it when they read the (appropriately edited) scene from Shakespeare.

The pebble-dash teacher who wants to explain everything in the scene will say that this approach doesn't provide enough learning, there's too much to get through to spend an hour on one or two ideas; and his pupils will go on making notes on a dozen things a day and when later asked what onomatopoeia is they will hesitate and then tentatively assert that it might be the one where all the words begin with the same letter.

Of course, focusing on one, two or three key objectives isn't limiting. The pupils are still learning about the plot of the play, the relationships within it; but the objectives provide a coherent

narrative to the stages of the lesson which gives them confidence. Because they understand ambiguity, they understand the scene; the objective is like a torch in the darkness, allowing the pupils to move forward and see more and more.

This lesson features role play and discussion work, but this shouldn't define it as an English lesson. Like most (arguably all) lessons, it's a literacy lesson. Concepts may be explored in these ways (as we've seen) in any secondary subject. We need to involve pupils in discussion and that discussion needs structures. I have listed in the preceding pages some structures for group discussions. One of the best and simplest structures I've ever seen is the dartboard.

Like the continuum (for/against...) mentioned above, the dartboard is a simple, graphic focus device. You draw a dartboard – some concentric circles; and pupils indicate opinions or predictions by placing marks on it. For example, whose fault is the tragedy in *King Lear*? Who caused the First World War? Pupils put the most blameworthy character in the middle, the least at the outside edge, and the others arranged between. They come to the main whiteboard and show what they think, disputing each other's positioning. The dartboard can be used to show any set of choices: likely outcomes or predictions, favourites and non-favourites, most important to least important. Of course, pupils can simply be asked to make lists; but there's something about the dynamic of the dartboard which focuses attention and demands argument.

What works well with the dartboard (or other similar discussion tool) is the progression from individual thought to pair work to whole-class discussion. This is an effective movement in your classroom. Each stage is managed and timed. Two or three minutes' silence, so people can have their own, original thoughts. Three minutes' pair discussion, where they can practise articulating their opinions. And then the whole-class discussion, where the central dartboard is marked and modified. This three-stage process is much more powerful than jumping unprepared straight to whole-class discussion. Any question-and-answer session works better when preceded by two minutes' silent jotting. For one thing, this empowers the teacher because children who've had thinking time can't opt out when asked to speak.

Most of this chapter so far centres on speaking and listening. It's sparse in some classrooms, and one way of developing your practice, with the potential for dramatic improvement, is in raising its status in your teaching. Of course, reading and writing are important too; often, they are the main focuses of school literacy policies.

Literacy: you as expert

I said in Chapter 1 that one of the dilemmas of teaching is the dilemma of expertise. You have to be subject expert, but you have to teach people who aren't and probably don't want to be. Remembering learning failures when you were at school is at least as important as remembering successes. Being good at it is easy. You have to imagine what it's like *not* to be good at it. Good teachers understand knowledge, but brilliant teachers understand ignorance.

Another area in which you are an expert is literacy. For example, you are an expert reader. You have a degree; you read all kinds of different texts to get it, and you learned all kinds of different ways of handling them. Adolescents don't have this experience base or this expertise. As always, we have to analyse our own implicit abilities and make them explicitly available to our pupils.

Consider, then, the things you can do with texts. You can understand the differences between them. You know which are deep and sustained and which are light and superficial. You know which are factual and which are contentious. You know which ones you really need and which you could manage without. You know how carefully you need to read. You know what you're reading for. You know that there are different kinds of reading. You know how to make notes. You know how to remember. You know how to select and discard.

Whatever your subject, you are a literacy expert. Of course, the things you 'know' listed above may not be things you think about; but it's fairly easy to consider ways of helping your pupils to make sense of their reading as you do.

For example, prediction activities, which we've already mentioned, are closely related to effective reading. Expert readers predict; as you read this sentence, you are predicting the end of it, and you are predicting the next sentence as well. Linear readers are weaker readers. Therefore, providing prediction exercises around texts is a powerful way of developing expert reading habits and thus progress within your subject. Such exercises are easy to devise. Various DARTs – such as sequencing, deletion exercises and sorting – invoke prediction and opinion.

I used to think that DARTs (*Directed Activities Related to Texts*) were puerile. I found them trendy and insulting. I was advised that I should cut up passages of text, or jumble them together, or draw pictures, or leave words out. I wrote it off as a *Blue Peter* approach to learning.

It is certainly true that these activities are pointless if they are introduced for the wrong reasons. Trainee teachers, when asked why they use a DART, will often reply that they want to make the work more interesting. Reading and making notes is *boring*; DARTs are more *exciting*. They are, in fact, *kinaesthetic*. None of this is sufficient reason for doing DARTs, or anything else, and indeed the word *kinaesthetic* is in danger of dying from exhaustion. I recently heard reading a novel described as a kinaesthetic activity – presumably because of the constant page-turning.

The DART is only effective when it makes sense of the text in terms of its key features. My own conversion to DARTs happened one afternoon on a teaching course, when I was given a scientific passage to make sense of. It was a description of the nitrogen cycle, in several paragraphs. The paragraphs were cut up and I had to sequence them. This is a basic and well-known DART. Any piece of text which has any kind of internal logic – description of process, of cause-and-effect, of narrative – can be subjected to this. In examining the logic of this piece of science, in piecing together this cycle which I knew very little about beforehand, I became analytically intimate with it. I came to understand the logic as I mined it for clues, as I attached each stage to the previous one. I pored over the nitrogen cycle in a way that I would never have done without the DART. I was converted by doing it; and, if you're sceptical, I implore you to try it for yourself. I've used DARTs ever since, and rarely do children get so close to and involved with text.

The DART introduces the element of game into the classroom, and this is always a good thing, though it's never the reason for using it. Just as some questions have right answers and some don't, and children need to know which they're dealing with, so some DARTs are open and some are closed. Remember, though, the reasons for doing them. If you've asked children to fill in blank words in a piece of text, you must have done it for a reason. Presumably, you want to draw attention to those words by making pupils think very hard about what they might be. At some point, you will tell them which words originally occupied those blank spaces and it's easy then for the lesson to turn into an auction, a brief frenzy about who got it right, pupils cheering or booing as each word is announced. It's likely, however, that 'getting it right' isn't the point. You may have run the DART so that pupils can be intrigued or surprised by the text, by the discovery that the original words are *not* the ones they chose. Indeed, if there is an outbreak of right answers, the children probably weren't challenged by the exercise. On such an occasion, what matters is the *comparison* between their words and the author's words. It's in this *comparison* that the value of the activity lies, though often the teacher doesn't address this at all. The 'right answers' are given, rendering the pupils' efforts and the DART largely redundant, and failing to close a powerful teaching-and-learning loop.

For example, you want to draw attention to an odd or unexpected outcome in a history lesson. People reacted to a historical event in a surprising way. Or the repercussions of a decision were not the ones expected or intended when the decision was made. Of course, you can *tell* pupils that the outcome was surprising, and, in a sense, they'll believe you. But if you first invite them – perhaps in pair discussion – to *predict* the outcome, they are unlikely to get it right. When they compare their own prediction with the reality (revealed by you), they will *know* how unexpected it is, because they didn't expect it themselves. They got your point by getting it *wrong*. The comparison between them and it forces the analysis. Similarly, the full drama of an unexpected end to a novel is brought home by prediction. At the end of Steinbeck's *Of Mice and Men*, George shoots his best friend Lennie in the back of the head (I'm sorry if I've spoilt it for you). For children, this is an astonishing ending. As anybody does when reading a story, they already have their views about how it should and will end. Comparing their predictions or opinions with the actual ending delivers all sorts of debate about surprise, structure and appropriateness. And it's very engaging work.

What else do you naturally do when you read that children need help with? You can make notes; but are you modelling this and helping pupils to see the range of different ways of doing it? By simply explaining that margin annotations cannot carry depth and detail and so must be supplemented by separate paper notes;

or by showing different note structures – mind-mapping, columns and so on – you can open people's eyes to the possibilities. And, of course, you are making them think about learning – so you are doing *meta-learning*. I once had a sixth-former come to me in tears because she couldn't make sense of her own notes. She'd been advised not to make notes in whole sentences – it was time-consuming – but, months later, she discovered that she couldn't understand a word. Students need to be advised to develop appropriate, varied and personal systems. For example, that particular student learned to check all notes two or three weeks after writing them and to adjust her compression accordingly. I warned all my students to develop a note-checking strategy as well as a note-making strategy.

You also know how to read. Children need this to be explained; they need to practise. This shouldn't be (and usually isn't) solely the work of the English department. Nor can it really have any life in 'study skills' sessions. You should be helping pupils to know whether to skim or scan or read deeply. Getting the gist in a short time is *skimming*. You can have fun with this; offer them a piece of subject text and do time trials on who can read and precis the main points the most quickly.

I have spent every New Year's Eve for the last thirty years with a group of increasingly ageing friends in someone's house. We sit and wait for the fireworks and we play games to pass the time – and, in recent years, to keep awake. Each year, one individual buys a pile of children's comics or, sometimes, the local paper. He buys twenty identical editions. He gives them out, and throws out questions – 'How old is Timothy Jenks?' 'What did Desperate Dan give to the burglar?'. We all desperately rifle through the papers, searching for the stories and the answers. This is *scanning*. Very similar games based around subject texts will help your children to learn its specific techniques and purposes. They need training, they need advising and, most of all, they need to understand that 'reading' isn't just one thing and that, sometimes, skimming or scanning isn't a sign of laziness, of work not properly done, but a conscious and appropriate choice. This is quite a liberating thought.

Here's a very simple and obvious thought. A great deal of what you read is forced upon you and, often, you're just looking for something. In effect, you're scanning. When reading a new piece of text, children need something to look for. A common (and ancient) model is to offer a portion of text followed by some questions about it – written or spoken. This was once known as 'comprehension' and is now largely discredited for a number of reasons, one of which was that you could often do it quite well without showing any comprehension at all. A much more productive and obvious model is to tell them what they're looking for *before* the reading. I do this always as a matter of course. It doesn't limit the reading; they will still see other things; but a focus – something to look out for – will keep them awake to the text.

Literacy: them as experts

But you aren't the only literacy expert in the room.

You particularly need children to be able to speak and write appropriately. They have to do these things in a range of formats and structures, for a range of purposes and for different audiences. They have to understand that writing the review of a piece of music is not the same as writing a fact-based piece about geography. Even within the same subject, you are making varying language demands on them. Sometimes (in history, for example) they need to be objective and crystal clear, and at other times they need to be evocative, imaginative and personal. These are quite sophisticated demands to make, but, when met, they pay off handsomely. Luckily, children already know a great deal about language structures.

For example, they know quite a lot about formal and informal writing. This understanding is probably important within your subject. When you're requiring them to be more formal, remember that it's not a new concept for them. Even if they've never been taught about it, even in English lessons, they already know it. They know that when they talk to you, the head teacher, their mum, their friends, they don't use the same language. They know that mixing this up can lead to bad results. Being over-familiar with teachers is likely to get you into trouble; being formal with mates will get you laughed at. Children know all this from quite early on. Rather that telling them what formal writing is (perhaps with a formal definition), try reminding them of the fact that language changes in these ways to suit audience. Defining the audience for a piece of subject writing is crucial to getting the tone right, and yet teachers rarely do it. They work on the basis that the audience – normally the teacher – is obvious. Varying the audience, so that pupils can learn to adapt their language, is easy and powerful. There are other audiences, real or imaginary: the local newspaper, examiners, other pupils, younger classes, their parents.

Consider the value of bringing these audiences into your classroom. As an evaluation (perhaps a plenary), you might ask pupils to summarise what they've learned. This is sensible, if deadly. Why not ask Year-10 to re-present their new understanding for a Year-7 class? In pairs, they work away at their new learning, stripping out irrelevancies and complexities, presenting a simplified, streamlined account which has required careful analysis, selection and judgement. If you can actually put this in front of Year-7, so much the better; but even if you can't, you can hear it presented within the classroom. They now have a purpose and focus for their summarising.

You can go further with this idea of purpose and audience. Children don't know much about essays but they are surrounded by text formats which they absolutely understand. I used to have them prepare radio news bulletins in groups. This is an English lesson (though it could certainly be successfully used in many other subjects). They write the bare bones of true news stories ('I did the washing up at the weekend'; 'My sister went out with her new boyfriend...'). These are torn up and thrown onto tables where groups have to form them into three-minute news bulletins.

The point of this work within English is that pupils understand the particular language of radio (or television) news. News programmes have their own rhythms, vocabulary and grammar. People are introduced formulaically ('Peter, 37, a joiner from Woodstock...'). Euphemisms and exaggerations are common. Connective links are essential ('Thank you, Lynne. Now over to Henry at the scene...'). News has specific vocabulary ('*Storm* over pay rise') that you would never use in real life. And the bulletin has a complex text-level structure, with levels of headline, hierarchical sequencing and clear closure ('and finally...'). To discover all this, I used to start this work by playing recordings of news programmes and analysing them with pupils. This is called *text-type analysis*. Having done the analysis, they would create their own programmes, using what they'd learned.

Or so I thought. In fact, the text-type analysis was virtually pointless. One day, on a whim, I ran the lesson without it. We looked at no samples; we just started by making our own bulletins. All of the news language was there. They already knew it. They are stuffed full with implicit understanding of how text structures work. They may not be exactly the structures they need to write in to pass their exams, but they are a constructivist starting point for understanding tone, audience and appropriateness. You can use them in your classroom to add variety, pace, interest and language awareness. In so doing, you will be using pupils as experts and reintroducing SFC.

We are talking in a sense about genre-awareness. Of course, children can produce information posters and leaflets, but it's worth considering the texts that surround them in their everyday lives. *Film trailers* are a potent summarising format. They can apply that ridiculous American baritone to brief but tantalising accounts of historical events or mathematical processes. They can devise *video simulation games* (they don't have to program them; they can just storyboard). Of course, they can make television *advertisements* or *game shows* based on international trade or global warming. In doing such work, they are becoming increasingly versatile about formats and so increasingly receptive to the idea of the range of structures and conventions that they need to use.

English as an additional language

EAL (like other forms of differentiation; see Chapter 6) is a problem. In England alone, we speak about 200 languages, and increasing numbers of our pupils don't speak much English. We know we should be doing more about it but, a lot of the time, we don't exactly know what. Possibly, admitting this difficulty is a starting point. You're a geography teacher, not an EFL teacher. And EAL most certainly isn't EFL anyway. You want to help these children. So what are you actually supposed to do?

Schools have extremely varied structural answers to this question. You may be working in an environment with a dedicated language unit or with specialist teaching assistants, or both. On the other hand, there are still UK schools with little or no formal EAL provision. So it's hard to generalise. Here's a basic position and a few basic suggestions to go with it.

You have to teach your subject. Perhaps that's a starting position: you're a maths teacher. You have to teach maths, not English, to pupils with EAL. This isn't an insensitive statement. If all subject teachers are trying to be amateur English teachers as well, confusion is a likely outcome (unless the school is significantly well-organised and the staff widely trained in EAL). But, given that this entire chapter is dedicated to the notion that language is the essential medium of teaching, we can't leave it there. You have to teach maths to pupils with EAL. You have little specialist understanding of language teaching and you don't speak Polish or Urdu. What does this all mean?

If you have help within the school, use it creatively. In terms of specialist assistance, for example, there are many effective ways of working collaboratively. There isn't only 'team-teaching' or one-to-one pupil support. Why not initiate real dialogue with your EAL teaching assistant? Ask her to observe your teaching. Ask her to evaluate it with you out of the classroom, to explain its impact (as she sees it) on your pupils with EAL. She is literally closer to them than you are. Ask her for suggestions for improvement. Teaching assistants can be a rich source of advice, especially with regard to the effects of your teaching on your pupils.

If you don't have much support, there are still things that you can do. I have seen several versions of EAL training material in which a group of UK 'pupils' (actually British trainee teachers from many subject disciplines) are taught physics by a teacher who speaks only German. Her 'pupils' speak little or no German. They aren't for the most part scientists, either. But after an hour, they have learned something. How can this be?

The teacher established a few simple language routines. She taught the class some procedural words in German: words for 'Sit down', 'Now you can start', 'Do you understand?' and so on. These were on a wall chart. There weren't many.

But the science teaching was inventive and differentiated. She:

- repeated selected key words and phrases;
- asked the pupils to repeat;
- asked the pupils to build lists of key words into personal dictionaries;
- modelled, using apparatus;
- showed connections by drawing on the board, for example by using arrows, spidergrams and sequences;
- sketched;
- demonstrated;
- used pair work, where pupils explained things to each other;
- asked pupils who understood something to explain it to others, encouraging them to use English (their home language) if necessary;
- offered a prepared writing frame for recording the experiment in German or English;
- wrote key German words on the board and spent time explaining them;
- set tasks that could be understood from practical modelling;
- set tasks that connected to each other obviously;
- gave plenty of time to transition periods;
- evaluated carefully, regularly and by practical methods where possible.

There is much support for your EAL teaching. There are websites where Local Authorities offer guidebooks for teachers and pupils. There are national diagnostic materials which can help you to assess pupils whose performance in English is below National Curriculum Level 1. The very useful QCA publication *A Language in Common* (QCA, 2000) offers a common scale for assessment which features levels defined as Step 1 and Step 2 below Level 1, and indeed Level 1 is split vertically in half. It also interestingly separates speaking from listening (which is not the case in the mainstream curriculum).

This talk of performance *below* Level 1 is of course accurate, but it's important to react appropriately to it. These pupils are often experienced and intelligent people. Their profile is sometimes uneven, and the separation of speaking and listening reflects this. They can be much better at one than the other, and this can be true either way round. Similarly, they may be much stronger at reading than writing, or vice versa. The profile may be more mixed than the profile of a home-English speaker. But it's not uncommon for them to be very proficient people and this can be (ironically) true in terms of their language ability. Given their life experiences, they may speak several languages quite well. They know how languages work and may well learn a new one quickly.

Whatever the level of support, in the end, you have to function in your classroom. The list of teaching approaches above isn't just a list of things to try when you have pupils whose main language isn't English. It's a list of lively, differentiated teaching methods which perhaps should be current in your classroom anyway, whatever the language issues. This is the beginning of a differentiated practice, and that, in its turn (as we will discuss in Chapter 6) is the key to brilliant teaching – because all teaching is mixed-ability teaching, and everyone has special needs.

Chapter 5

The paradox of inspiration

I once heard a child say about me, 'He's all right. You have a laugh, but he makes you work' and, to my chagrin, I've remembered this with pleasure for about thirty years. This is partly because you don't get many compliments in this job, but I believe it's also because it contains the germ of quite an important idea about inspirational teaching. It's a sort of paradox, and in that respect it echoes other things we say about good teachers – for example, the old cliché about being *firm but fair*.

I remember also a brief conversation when I was planning the A-level teaching for my department. We taught in pairs, and two of my staff commented that they knew why I always put them together. 'Amy's the creative one,' Chris said, 'and I'm very reliable. If you could put us together, you'd have one really good teacher.'

Of course, the danger with *firm but fair* and similar pairings is that they can sound like a sort of middle way, a sort of Social-Democratic approach to teaching. *I'm in the middle, I'm at neither extreme...* This sounds like a comfortable position. It's probably better than being stuck out at one end or the other. But, as the old joke goes, the middle of the road actually isn't a very safe place. It's possible to be offering neither one thing nor the other.

You know about all those extremes. They surround behaviour-management attitudes. They surround subject issues. As an English teacher, I was frequently accosted by people at parties who asked me which end of the spectrum I was at. Was I a creative teacher? Creative teachers apparently think that spelling doesn't matter. They are also the people who encourage children to mug little old ladies in the name of self-expression. Hollywood and the tabloid press play a part in this nonsense. Or was I a back-to-basics man, who operated in rows, in black-and-white and in the subjunctive? It's hard to say that you're both; it's tempting to retreat to the centre ground, and try a little of everything.

The good teacher runs in the middle, or perhaps works one half of the paradox to advantage, but the brilliant teacher reconciles the extremes. This makes her practice varied, differentiated, energetic, robust and exciting. It is based on what Charles Atlas, a mail-order fitness guru of the 1950s, would have called 'dynamic tension'. Anyone can do it, but it isn't easy and it needs thinking about.

You might like to consider the paradoxes below. You could position yourself within them. Do you tend towards one end or the other? Or do you inhabit the middle ground? How could you extend your practice to embrace both extremes?

Inspirational teaching is, for example:

- focused but divergent;
- creative but directed;
- sustained but eventful;
- planned but spontaneous;
- expert but interactive;
- abstract but concrete;
- general but specific.

Let's take some of these and consider what, in practical terms, they might mean.

Focused but divergent

Focus is a key planning virtue. It begins, of course, with the learning objectives. Lessons need two or three learning objectives and these need to be specific and local. They are published to the pupils and frequently referred to. The more crafted they are, in terms of a particular teaching group on a particular day, the more focus you have; and the more purposeful and secure will be the learning.

In the planning, this can translate into focusing devices. Any kind of writing frame or prompt script offers focus. Concrete (rather than abstract) questions offer strong starting focus. Graphical focuses include the continua and dartboards that we discussed in the previous chapter. Careful selection of material is crucial to focus.

A teacher with a high level of focus sticks to the point. The children understand the learning and there is a strong sense of direction. The lesson isn't derailed and the momentum is strong. Children respond to this level of security and premeditation, and it puts the teacher in a very strong place. But there is little flexibility or responsiveness in this teaching.

The *divergent* teacher is ready to take a detour. One type of divergence is based on response; the lesson takes an unexpected turn because an interesting discovery is made, because a child makes an idiosyncratic contribution, because someone turns out to be an expert, or because the class doesn't understand what's happening. Rather than plodding on regardless, the divergent teacher recognises cues and makes changes. He is on constant evaluative alert. But being divergent is more than just being prepared to change if necessary. It involves planning range and individuality into the lesson. This teacher offers a range of access routes to the learning, explaining things in different ways, working in response to learning styles. There is variety and surprise in the room, but sometimes there is a lack of purpose or authority. Sometimes, there is a lack of planning.

What we want is to be both; we want to be Amy *and* Chris. For convenience, I'm going to call this reconciliation *dynamic* teaching. In this case, the dynamic reconciling of these opposites lies in the relationship of the general and the specific. It begins with having a strong focus but being prepared to digress where necessary; but it's considerably more than this. The divergence isn't an unexpected breakdown of the plan; it's part of it.

A geography teacher wants children to see what type of town they live in. He talks to them about it, and he shows them photographs which indicate that it's a port. We have reflected on such a lesson in previous chapters and we commented that comparison is a constant teaching strength. The definitions sharpen up if there is more than one type of town on the table.

The teacher who believes that he is teaching just about one town is the focused teacher; but in doing that teaching, he may be neglecting significant learning. The children need to understand the notion of there being different sorts of towns before they can confidently define their own. So divergence from the central focus – Swansea – is necessary. The specific learning needs a generalised context, or it may make no sense. Children have to learn both that we define towns in terms of types and how we do that. This lesson needs opening activities, based on comparisons, which will establish that context.

How do you manage divergence without losing focus? You need clear planning decisions about how the general relates to the specific, and you need instruments and lesson resources to do this. For example, how do we classify a town? We might look at its size, its location, the way it makes its money, what people living there spend their time doing. We are now building a general checklist for town-type classification. This can be presented to children. In the left-hand column are these categories. The right-hand column is blank. In a sense, this looks like a list of questions, with blank spaces for answers, and we may be tempted, therefore, to believe that the right-hand column is where the learning is. Swansea is a port; that's what we've learned. It's in the right-hand column. It's a fact. But the left-hand column is vital to the learning, because that's where we're learning not about Swansea but about how we talk about towns – how geography works.

With this simple resource – a checklist, or prompt script – pupils can look at *any* town. In a single lesson, they might research all sorts of towns. They might be allowed to choose a town with which they have some connection – they were born there, their grandparents live there, they go there on holiday. Or they might be allocated various towns. Each one has a different town; but they all have the same checklist. The checklist holds the pupils to a common focus – how we talk about towns – and the variety allows for divergence, comparison and discovery. It's this relationship between a broad range of material and a single, central focusing device that allows children to foster their own understanding and geographical skill. And we have a dynamic and differentiated lesson.

In English, we want pupils to study magazines. We want them eventually to create their own magazines, or at least their own magazine covers. (This is in itself a focusing device. They can learn a great deal about print media from the cover alone, and, compared to making the entire magazine, this focus allows for concentration.) Why are we doing this? Are we training pupils to become magazine editors or graphic designers? No; we are teaching them that media texts have their own conventions, purposes and audiences. They have their own techniques and terminology. Children are learning to be sophisticated and critical media consumers. That's a worthwhile learning objective.

Before designing their own magazines, children are likely to look at examples of real ones. I've done this dozens of times. You hand out photocopies of a single magazine, so that you are all looking at the same thing, and you can guide the class through a shared analysis. You can define key terms about a magazine cover (they have straps, puffs and pugs, among other things). You can talk about the magazine title, the cover imagery, the fonts, the colours, the intended audience. Using a single magazine facilitates this analysis. It creates focus. But it might, in the end, mean that pupils are learning about one magazine rather than about how magazines work in general.

A more divergent approach is to hand out many different magazines. You might allow pupils to bring in their favourites. This supports the idea of studying magazines as a genre, rather than studying just one. It allows the discovery of common themes among varied materials. But now children might just sit there turning pages in the sort of distracted trance that magazines are designed to induce. And the shared analysis is much more difficult to achieve with such divergence of examples in the room.

Once again, you need a central focusing device. A sheet of

prompts, which everyone shares, allows them to get on with the analysis. Now they are working (perhaps) on magazines that interest them, that they've chosen. They are in a classroom where many comparisons can be made. They are learning that there are common techniques and motives behind these apparently dissimilar things. They are learning about publishing.

So the dynamic teacher uses simple classroom resources to mix focus with range. In fact, the magazine lesson goes further. The analysis sheet used here is adapted from Literacy Framework materials. Children complete it with regard to their chosen magazines. But in future lessons, the same analysis sheet can re-appear and support the analysis of advertisements, news bulletins, book covers, information leaflets, holiday brochures. The range becomes ever broader, but the constancy of the analysis sheet gives centre to the range and reminds children that all of these disparate texts are doing pretty much the same things. In returning to it they are developing their analytical powers and their confidence. They are understanding processes.

One structural approach to divergence (and to creativity; see below) is cross-curricularity. As we said in Chapter 4, it has a chequered history. It seems to hover as a sort of conscience-appeaser. We know that there should be links between subjects, but we have our expertises and our timetables, so we work out themes and audits. This is often a compromise. It may work, but it may become a nuisance. I remember several years of having to fend off the history department, explaining that children couldn't be taught Shakespeare at a particular time just because they were doing Elizabethan England in history, and that, even though Year-7 were ready for the First World War, they weren't ready for Wilfred Owen.

Cross-curricularity (like creativity) is thankfully on the move in UK secondary teaching, and we have opportunities now to explore ways of making it work; of making it active, meaningful and successful. Of course, some subjects – English and art, geography and history, maths and music, music and art, and so on – naturally fit together. But why not try something more ambitious?

The best cross-curricular work I've seen was a three-day off-timetable sixth-form conference. It had a single, well-chosen focus: it was on Darwin and evolution. The organisation centred on expert speakers (from the school but also the local university) and break-out discussion groups. It culminated in a plenary question-time panel of all the speakers.

Table 5.1 Text-type analysis

Text type	
Purpose	
• What is its purpose?	
• Who is it for?	
• How will it be used?	
• What kind of writing is therefore appropriate?	
Text level	
• Layout	
• Structure/organisation	
• Sequence	
Sentence level	
• Viewpoint	
• Prevailing tense	
• Active/passive voice	
• Typical sentence structure and length	
• Typical cohesion devices	
Word level	
• Stock words and phrases	
• Specialised or typical vocabulary	
• Elaborate/plain vocab choices	
Other typical features:	
How could this text be improved?	
Personal reactions to the text:	

The point of the conference was that the notion of evolution created a seismic cultural shock, and this reverberated in all the corners of society. So it wasn't just a scientific discovery; it had implications across all disciplines – and all A levels.

There were talks on:

- the context: scientific and cultural attitudes before Darwin;
- biology before and after Darwin;
- geology and palaeontology;
- cosmology (versions of the universe from ancient times, and how they reflected the cultures that made them);
- literature (poetry and novels changed after Darwin. Wordsworth couldn't have written *The Daffodils* after Darwin);
- music (the retreat from romanticism);
- religion (how did personal faith and the Church cope with this new view of creation?);
- philosophy (man's privileged position has been undermined);
- psychology (Darwin and Freud: a new view of man);
- language (Darwin changed the language. 'Survival of the fittest' is one of the most abused and misunderstood phrases in English);
- history (there were many changes. Business changed; politics changed).

This conference was very successful. Years later, those sixth-formers were still saying to me that this was a major event in their education; because it was the first time that they had genuinely understood all of those connections; that science affected poetry; that music reflected history. In other words, cross-curricularity actually meant something. Of course, it was well-planned and the speakers well-chosen; but it worked because it had a clear and well-chosen focus. It ranged widely across many subject disciplines but it never lost its centre, and so the comparisons and the enrichment were irresistible. Structurally (and appropriately) it abandoned the subject-driven timetable – an arrangement that was both practical and symbolic.

This business of *focus* is worth a little more thought. Focus enables breadth, rather than restricting it. If you still have a manual-focus camera, you will know that when you look through the viewfinder at a landscape you want to photograph, you adjust the focus by concentrating on a single item. You pick out a tree or a building, and you focus on that. This brings the whole landscape into sharp relief; but it's done by close concentration on one thing.

In fact, the word *concentration* is also worth a moment's thought. It's what we want children to do – we say, 'For heaven's sake, Laura, *concentrate*!'. We regret their ever-shortening *concentration span*. Concentrating is a good thing.

But in usage, concentration is virtually (though not actually) two words. It has an alternative meaning, applied to soup or fruit juice. A concentration (or concentrate) is a reduction to the essence. It may be helpful to reconnect these two uses of the same word. If we want to support pupils' concentration, perhaps we need to help them with that reduction, to encourage focus on the magazine cover rather than the whole magazine, on a key aspect, on the tree rather than the whole landscape. Focusing devices are selections that we make which concentrate the minds of our pupils.

Creative but directed

These pairings echo each other. Once again, we are dealing here with range (on the one hand) and purpose (on the other). Let's spend another minute defining creativity. One of the problems in seeking this dynamic tension is the notion that creativity knows no bounds. It can't be directed. It depends on absolute personal freedom. Creative writing is the unfettered expression of the individual psyche. You can't objectify it. So you can't direct it.

I don't offer this version of creativity sarcastically. I think there's something in it. Our objectives-driven curricula don't make enough room for it; but that's no reason to abandon creativity. For one thing, there's more than one sort.

It might help to set the conventional image of the creative artist, alone and suffering in a garret, against other versions of creativity. What does a truly creative *footballer* do? Does he abandon the offside rule altogether, or decide that it's okay to carry the ball in his hands from time to time? He expresses his creativity *through* the rules, not despite them. If there were no rules, there would be no game, and he would have to take his creativity somewhere else. (I suppose he might invent rugby, but that's another, very untypical story.) Oxbridge candidates are offered the essay question, 'What do you think about music?'. At first glance, they are relieved; they haven't been asked about some obscure composer they've never heard of. With a smile, they consider what to write. And they go on considering, as time ticks away, and the panic of unstructured freedom begins to set in.

So there can be a relationship between structure and creativity – between the river and the banks. The dynamic teacher builds creativity into lessons, without losing the overall direction. We can think of creativity in terms of group work, problem-solving, prediction, rather than pure aesthetics. The direction, the aim of the lesson isn't negotiated; but the route is up for grabs. The clarity of direction frames the creativity.

A television reality show offers potential chefs a pile of ingredients. They all have the same ingredients, but they can cook what they like. There are more ingredients than they need, so an early decision is which ones to use and which to discard. Imagine a science, art or design and technology lesson like this. Pupils design or construct something from a range of given materials. In making those initial decisions – what to make, what to use, what not to use – they have to become very close to the capabilities of those materials and to the appropriate design and construction processes.

Teachers in the UK feel (I suspect) wearily ironic about recent calls for more creativity in our work – from the very establishment which spent the last twenty-five years eradicating it. It doesn't sit easily with a testing regime. But we welcome it, nevertheless. It can appear in many guises. Often, creativity is concerned with

coincidence, or accident. At a creative writing workshop, the children write everyday objects – *pen, sun, dog* – on cards. The cards are randomly paired and the children have to write comparisons – similes, in effect – based on the pairings. How is a *horse* like a *soldier*? They start with an accident, and make something – sometimes, something quite insightful or beautiful. This notion of accident, of arbitrary, perhaps random starting points, is available in any lesson. Ask children to solve mathematical, historical or scientific problems, and give them some random tools to work with. What they have to do is create a solution out of the accident – to make the best of what they have, to turn a negative into a positive. Escaping prisoners of war (I believe) made authentic-looking identity documents and banknotes out of blankets and mattresses. The restrictions demanded true creativity. I would imagine that any employer would be very enthusiastic about school leavers with such abilities.

Children could be asked to write a love poem. They'll have a go, but they won't know where to start. This openness may support creativity, but it may simply be inhibiting. On the other hand, they could be asked to write a sonnet. A sonnet is an odd, ridiculous thing to adolescents. It has fourteen lines (why not twelve, or fifteen?) and a fairly crippling rhyme and rhythm scheme. But the arbitrary structure – the restriction – forces a kind of concentration, and children struggling within it make unexpected discoveries and unforeseen solutions. For example, the peculiar requirements of the rhyming system force them into finding new words. They are moved beyond the trite and into new ways of thinking. Constriction demands creative escape.

There are problems with the testing culture and creativity. For one thing, it isn't easy to test in a conventional sense. I spent years marking English Literature papers which allowed for creative (or 'recreative') answers. Instead of writing an essay about *The Merchant of Venice*, you would pretend you were Shylock and write about your feelings. It became very clear to me that, though these activities are excellent in the classroom, they do not sit well in a standard examination context. A hot afternoon in the school hall, and your future life depending on it, is not a great place for creativity. More to the point, it's virtually impossible to assess it in that way.

I think that the testing culture is even more insidious in terms of creativity when it generates a classroom atmosphere that only values right answers. This is where we must attack the problem. The single most beneficial thing we can do to foster creativity is to see it not as some odd, aesthetic indulgence but as part of everyday life and every lesson. To do this, we must establish a classroom that values experiment and collaboration. If you do a DART (see Chapter 4) which, for example, involves children filling in blanks, remember that the point of the activity is not to test them (a cheer for every right answer) but to compare their words with the original words, so approaching an understanding of the text. The whole business of rewarding right answers has no part in this kind of activity. There is a world of difference between saying, 'No, that's not it' and saying, 'Well, the text says something else. But let's look at why you wrote that...'. When you do the latter, you are actually being constructivist; you are leading the child from where he is to where you want him to be, and he is part of that progress. And you are building a classroom where everyone is prepared to experiment.

Is this in defiance of the testing regime? Personally, I wouldn't mind if it were. The whole thing is falling increasingly into disrepute, and I hope that disrepair and abandonment will follow. But, in fact, I don't think it needs to be at odds with testing. Creativity engenders confidence, versatility and intellectual agility. These are major assets to pupils when they're taking examinations.

Sustained but eventful

I see these two sorts of lessons very often. Sometimes, they relate to two sorts of teacher, but it's also quite common for one teacher to do both at different times. Sustained teaching is getting on with it. It's Shape A of our lesson shapes in Chapter 3. You do your coursework; you work through the exercises; we read a text together, making notes as we go. There is solid process here, but nothing inspirational or memorable is likely to happen. Events are memorable things. I once asked my Upper Sixth which lessons they remembered from the previous year. After a pause, they agreed on a particular Chaucer lesson. I was pleased. 'Why do you remember that?' I asked. 'Because it was hot, and we went outside', they replied.

I remembered it then, too. It wasn't a great lesson. In fact, going outside because it's a nice day is almost never a good idea. But, like them, I couldn't remember any other individual lessons.

Of course, this doesn't mean that we learned nothing from those forgotten lessons, but the problem with the *sustained* model – and it can go on for terms – is that learning may stop framing itself and announcing itself. It may stop burrowing into your pupils' minds. You sit in a quiet room. Suddenly, the heating switches off. The sound of the electric fan stops, and you notice that sound then for the first time. Until a change happens, the sustained noise becomes inaudible. Sustained teaching can fade away.

Of course, we need *sustained*. We need sustenance. When we're doing coursework, sometimes all we really want to say is, 'Get on with it.' We may present it better, but that's what we're saying. But if we're saying it too often (more than once a week), we may have to revise our approach. We have to create events. We can't just pour out the gin and tonic and leave it standing for hours on end. It becomes undrinkable. We have to freshen it up with more tonic, more ice or more gin. Children need refocusing, the course-work needs revitalising; and there are many ways of doing this. Introduce new themes or suggestions from time to time. Do a piece of peer assessment from time to time. Show them the assessment objectives and have them revise their recent work in the light of them. Have periodic show-and-tell sharing sessions. Have paired interventions, where they try to solve each other's problems. Show them some good and bad examples. Stop the process and run class lessons – speaking and listening lessons, discussing key issues arising from the coursework. The dynamic teaching programme matches the strength of sustained continuity with regular moments of new focus or refocus. Whether in the individual lesson (often in the form of transitions; see Chapter 3) or across the scheme of work, there need to be peaks.

Planned but spontaneous: expert but interactive

My argument is that, if you want to be brilliant, not planning isn't an option. Not having learning objectives isn't an option (they're there to learn, not to do). But of course abandoning either is always an option, and sometimes the best lessons happen as a result. A difficult, low-ability Year-10 becomes voluble about something that's only tangentially related to the lesson. Or a high-ability Year-11 becomes fascinated by what you'd thought of as

an aside. At that point you make the decision – should I go with this? The making of relationships is a slow business. It isn't achieved by instant rapport and charisma but by the subliminal building of respect over months. Sometimes, a lesson may be sacrificed or enhanced by shifting the agenda. There are rules here, of course. The decision must be yours and must be seen to be so. But the lesson plan isn't a straitjacket.

In the UK, the secondary frameworks and strategies favour *interactive* teaching. It's a much-used term, but it requires some definition, and we must think hard about our own teacherly role with regard to it.

I watch lessons often where the activity level is high. There are felt-tips and computers. There is group and pair work. There is plenty of talk. The teacher asks lots of questions. It can happen, however, that not much learning actually gets done. The lesson product can be surprisingly minimal. 'I don't get it,' says the disappointed teacher, afterwards. 'It was a really interactive lesson.'

There are reasons for the failure of such a lesson. It's possible that it wasn't very interactive at all. It's a much misused term. It doesn't just mean *active*. Of course, it concerns the spoken relationship between the teacher and the children, and it's propounded as good practice because it's intended to reduce bulky teacher-talk sessions and put children into the conversation in a social-constructivist way. Often, however – even in strategy training materials – it's shown to be very active, lively question-and-answer sessions. The teacher has his questions, he asks them with energy, children volunteer, the atmosphere feels co-operative and successful. How *interactive* is this?

I'm arguing that if the teacher simply asks his questions and takes answers (possibly with too much YAVA, but that's another point), he's being active, but he isn't being *interactive*. Interactivity isn't just noise and bubble; interactivity is by definition a mutual business. The truly interactive teacher is on evaluative alert. He listens to every answer, and he *modifies his questions and his teaching in the light of the answers and the understanding that they show*. This is when it stops being a game ('guess the answer!') and becomes a developmental conversation between teacher and class. Interactivity isn't just the children talking a lot – it's the teacher listening a lot.

Of course you are an interactive teacher – how could you not be? And part of that role involves listening and modifying, as you do in any conversation. In fact, there are very few conversations outside the classroom which insist on sticking to a prepared plan. If your wife or boyfriend says something interesting over dinner, you don't just ignore it and move on to the next question on your list. I have been part of job interview panels where we were all required to ask the same pre-planned questions of all candidates. This was intended to promote equal opportunities – which, of course, is precisely what it *didn't* do. A candidate offering a piece of interesting and relevant information would find it bewilderingly ignored while we asked about something else. Classrooms seem to be one of the few places where we habitually define conversation in this way. A conversation is only interactive when it departs from the plan.

I see many exciting, interactive lessons where the teacher is listening, reworking, modifying, redefining, refining spontaneously. He's sticking to the direction of his plan but he's constantly shifting the language he's using to get there. In these lessons, the learning becomes a joint activity – and this is the holy grail of teaching. But in all this activity, it's possible for the teacher's own role to be lost. Many lessons are planned around pupils' activity. First they will do this, then this, and finally this… It's a common and

reasonable way of thinking about how a lesson looks. It's certainly valid and essential planning. Increasingly, however, teachers leave something out. They don't plan *themselves* into the lesson.

The reason often given for this is self-effacing – *I don't want to talk too much... I want it to come from them...* Of course, we can conventionally think of two types of teacher. One stands at the front and tells children what to think. Everyone respects him for his subject knowledge but it's generally accepted that he's boring, he can't 'get it across', he doesn't have much interest in the children. And then there's the teacher who's always on the move, never at the front, always asking, always listening, often kneeling and supporting individuals. We warm to the second stereotype, although we feel an odd sort of regret about the first one. But the fact is, they are both stereotypes, and the second one is no more complete as a teacher than the first.

The danger of interactivity is that, in properly placing children at the centre of the conversation, and indeed establishing them as experts, the teacher risks abandoning her own status. She risks becoming (as we said briefly in Chapter 1) an administrator of her own lessons. She must remain the expert. She establishes and guides the learning, and the children want this and are grateful for it. This doesn't mean that she delivers lectures, but it means that there are key lesson moments and key lesson ideas where she mustn't be afraid to take charge. Increasingly often, this doesn't happen. The children are set interesting tasks, but they struggle with them because certain key ideas have been taken for granted. They mustn't be.

Here's an example from a Media lesson I watched recently. It was a very well-planned lesson, based on the film *Shrek*. The resources were focused, the objectives clear on the lesson plan. The children were comparing *Shrek* to a conventional fairy tale. They were doing this with well-prepared prompt scripts which invited them to work on key characters. The scripts couldn't have been better. They listed character categories (such as *appearance*, *attitude*, *mission*) and put these into columns for conventional fairy-tale characters and for characters from *Shrek*. The children, who had watched the film, began work on these sheets.

The task-setting here consisted of handing out the sheets and explaining the mechanics of completing them. There was no QDO, minimal teacher-talk, and no settling period with the teacher at the front of the room. Once they started, the children began to struggle. They didn't understand the basic concept of the comparison. The idea is that *Shrek* is a modern take on a fairy tale; it twists some of the conventions; the modern characters are more mixed and comical than the old ones. The lesson material was wholly appropriate to this, but the idea itself had never been explained. The teacher has the idea, designs careful, scaffolded materials, and *expects the resources to bear the explanation*. Discovery is great, but explorers need guides as well as maps.

In fact, what happened in that lesson – and this happens so often – is that the teacher had to stop the activity and explain. She had to press the re-set button. She had been answering so many queries that she realised something was wrong. It hadn't occurred to her in her planning that she would need to chat to the whole class about this idea of a modern twist on an old story. It's an easy idea, and there are plenty of examples of it around in the children's lives – in television adverts, for example, or computer games. She didn't need to lecture, and was of course quite right not to; but *she did need to deal proactively with key ideas with the whole class.*

It's almost a geographical point. Interactive whiteboards, differentiation and interactivity in general have almost displaced the teacher from the centre-front. Because this is so good in so many ways, we may be in danger of losing the residual virtues of being visible, being authoritative (not authoritarian), being where we can monitor everybody. Modern teachers don't and shouldn't stand at the front and lecture. But they mustn't lose sight of the importance of teaching the whole class.

Marrying the two approaches is simple enough. The dynamic teacher is highly interactive and respectful of children's expertise. She spends most of her time in the body of the classroom supporting individuals and groups. But she isn't embarrassed to deal with the whole class at key, transitional moments, and she understands that task-setting is about ideas as well as explanations and instructions. The rhythm of her lesson is varied between the two types of conversation and the children understand this, and are more secure and focused for it. In fact, she explains to them as she moves from one mode to the other – 'Now, you've listened to me for a couple of minutes, and it's time for some group discussion. So things will get a bit noisier now, for the next eight or nine minutes...'. All of this is enabled, of course, in the preparation, when *the teacher introduces herself and her words back into the lesson plan.*

Abstract but concrete: general but specific

Some teachers are good at details and some are better at overview. The dynamic teacher moves frequently from one to the other. The abstract is where the conceptual learning is, but the concrete is where the understanding begins to develop. Difficult ideas are grown, not taught, and the growth may be the journey from the concrete to the abstract.

In fact, it's possible to consider this as a lesson template. We start concrete, because it's where the children are. Concrete is personal anecdote, example, experience. It's stories. In Chapter 3 we suggested that opening activities may not be defining activities. They may be concrete activities which begin the journey. These are the lesson foothills. We must begin there, because we can all step onto the foothills, hardly realising we're doing it. We examined a maths lesson on *symmetry*. Symmetry is an abstract concept, but we began by exemplifying it concretely. The children move towards the concept, but we have also pushed the concept towards them by this concrete rendering. Consider how far such learning can travel. If you have the concrete foundation (to coin a phrase) you can build very high. A gifted child who begins with that graphical image of symmetry – marks opposite each other on a whiteboard – can move beyond maths. Imagine that pupil talking about the symmetry of a piece of music, a poem, or a political argument. She can do that because somewhere within her remains that picture of balance, that concrete anchor.

If you try to begin abstract you risk a non-starter, a tumbleweed moment. When teaching Steinbeck's *Of Mice and Men* to Year-10, I want them to understand the part that dreams play in the characters' lives. George and Lennie are poor itinerant workers who dream together of owning a little house, with vegetables and rabbits in the garden. They repeat this dream to each other throughout the book. I want pupils to understand its significance – that their dream consistently reveals what's lacking in their world. This is an abstract idea, and some of the detail within it is abstract, too. Why do they want rabbits? Because Lennie wants to love rabbits; but also because he needs to be responsible for something. Rabbits are concrete, but responsibility is abstract.

There are ways of beginning which are unlikely to work. I have my objective: that children will understand the significance of the dream in the book. I have recognised (as we said in Chapter 2) that there is actually more than one objective there. Before they can apply it to the book, they have to understand in general terms that dreams reveal truths. This objective-splitting is always a good thing because it reveals the steps of the learning and supports your staged planning. But it means that we have generalisations to deal with, and that's a problem, because children are more comfortable with specifics.

What won't work is if I open with the main question – 'What are dreams for?'. If you're lucky, this may occasionally elicit a constructive answer, but it's more likely to fail. Could you answer it? It's abstract, and it's mysterious – what sort of answer are you looking for? Children spend a lot of time working out not what they think, but what they think you want them to say. As well as abstract, this question is impersonal. It's always a good idea to start personal. Adolescents are interested in themselves.

So I could ask, 'Why do *you* dream?', which is more personal but still abstract. What I actually ask is, 'What did you dream about last night?'. The conversation then moves from the personal to the formal and from the concrete to the abstract as we listen to anecdotes and see if we can see any patterns.

Such a movement is supported by lesson materials such as the *I dream of/I lack* table (Table 5.2) which, by using a blend of pupil opinion, example and material based on the Steinbeck text easily underpins a progression. If you dream of a hi-fi, you lack a hi-fi; but if you dream of a holiday, it's not because you lack a holiday. The concrete *hi-fi* answer leads almost imperceptibly to the abstract *holiday* answer (you dream of a holiday, you lack freedom, relaxation, independence, adventure – we are now effortlessly into abstract territory). And working from pupils' anecdotal experience seamlessly into the Steinbeck – on the same worksheet – attaches study to real life.

So abstract concepts need to be kick-started by concrete activity, and then regularly punctuated by it. Reminders of the original work – the symmetry diagram, the *I dream of/I lack* table – refocus strugglers and stragglers and support high-flyers. These are complex relationships, but they can be managed, so long as they are planned.

This reconciling of opposites into a dynamic practice isn't easy;

Table 5.2 I dream of / I lack

I dream of	I lack
a hi-fi	a hi-fi
a pet	warmth companionship
a holiday	rest adventure excitement

George and Lennie dream of	They lack
rabbits	warmth companionship responsibility hope
a stove	warmth stability self-sufficiency decent food
a house	pride status stability autonomy comfort
land	food comfort status independence freedom

it's done by planning. It might also help to reflect on features of your teaching personality. For example, I feel ready to do this balancing partly because I think it reflects my character. I am a cynical idealist, and my approach to teaching probably reflects this. Technically, I suppose I'm an oxymoron (you could insert your own joke here); perhaps everyone is. I'm romantic about how things ought to be; but I'm cynical about how they actually are. Consequently I'm happy to set lofty aims against pragmatic realities. As teachers, we need to define ourselves. Perhaps we all need to find this duality, this tension within ourselves, because it creates energy. Deft movement between opposites doesn't happen by chance. It happens as a result of self-awareness and careful planning. And when it does happen, the learning is dynamic, secure and meaningful.

Chapter 6

A differentiated practice

Differentiation is one area where, as an experienced teacher, you can get better – because progress here is virtually infinite. It's important, we do a lot of work with it, but we always feel that we could do more. In this sense, it can be a source of guilt (and guilt is a very teacherly emotion). It's a matter of common sense that efficient teaching takes account of the varying personalities of those who are learning. You have twenty-eight pupils with twenty-eight reading ages, personal histories, individual needs, numeracy levels, learning styles, interests, SAT scores, CAT scores, attitudes and preferences, and some of those have changed since last week. And you have four classes a day. They are all mixed-ability classes, because all classes are mixed-ability classes (children don't come in ability-batches of twenty-eight); and a good deal of differentiation isn't just about ability anyway. You know that differentiation is more than graded worksheets. The challenge and pressure of all this is enormous and we need to seek realistic solutions.

The first thing that you could do is to take stock of where you are. You are already differentiating. For example, do you:

- *talk to individuals about their work* in any context? Do you discuss their coursework drafts with them? Do you work on their reading choices in the LRC?
- *always QDO?*
- *give some extra explanation*, perhaps during a QDO session when task-setting, or in response to a pupil question?
- *vary class questioning*, for example by avoiding YAVA?
- *give pupils time to discuss tasks in pairs*, perhaps as part of QDO?

- *write comments on children's work*, addressing its strengths, suggesting improvements and developments, and engaging with the content?
- *ask the class questions*, for example during a plenary or a lesson transition?
- *answer pupil questions*, and make spaces for them to ask?
- *assess pupils' work*?
- *provide a variety of resources*?
- *use pupils as experts*, for example by allowing them to plan presentations on their own subject enthusiasms?
- *allow peer assessment* from time to time, so that pupils see (or hear) and discuss each other's work? (See *Assessment for learning*, Chapter 8.)
- *have group discussion*?
- *allow pupils to work in areas of personal interest*?
- *give a choice of tasks* from time to time; for example, allowing groups to choose their feedback method, or allowing individuals to choose their text type (poster, leaflet, newspaper letter)?
- *use a variety of activities* to move towards your learning objectives?
- *explain things two or three ways*?
- *set research homeworks*?

- set 'family' homeworks, such as interviewing your Mum about her favourite music?
- chat?
- praise?
- ask for pupil opinions on an issue or a text, and perhaps list and discuss those opinions?
- run interactive starters?
- work collaboratively with the whole class, for example on a shared writing exercise?
- work with selected groups, for example on shared reading?
- work with Learning Support Assistants, including briefing and debriefing them?
- work with computers?
- use an interactive whiteboard, for example to note and print pupil contribution?
- do pair work?
- evaluate learning and modify your teaching?
- encourage pupils to keep a subject log? (See Assessment for learning, Chapter 8.)

You will notice two things about this list. First, although it's a list of differentiation routines, it's also a list of good classroom practices. Good teaching and differentiation are almost synonymous. The second thing is that you can answer 'Yes' to virtually all of these questions. This isn't a list of new suggestions; it's an account of your existing practice and its purpose is to remind you that you are already differentiating on a regular basis. Nevertheless, to be brilliant, you may need to develop this good practice and to make it more explicit.

No doubt you are involved (perhaps with colleagues) in preparing differentiated materials and work schemes. By the way, you need to consider how they will be targeted and monitored. It's not unusual to see great efforts being made in resource creation undermined by quite crude classroom deployment in terms of who does what and why, often based solely on rough-and-ready notions of ability. This is long-term work and an important focus of activity within a teaching department. Meanwhile, let's consider some more immediate ways of building differentiation.

There are, of course, well-documented categories of differentiation, such as differentiation by *task*, by *outcome*, by *resource*, by *support* and by *response*, and these are partly covered by the list above. We've also already covered some significant differentiation practices in earlier chapters, and that's hardly surprising, since issues of learning focus and management naturally involve differentiation. For example, in Chapter 4, we talked in detail about *teacher language*. The conscious, planned use of varied tones and registers in teacher explanations is a powerful and immediately available tool of differentiation. Teachers sometimes spend months developing excellent resources but not even a few minutes planning how to talk to children about them. Remember: you need variety, examples, range and imagery when you talk to children.

Another obvious and direct route to differentiation is *pupil choice*, and we talked about this in Chapter 3. I personally still remember two things that happened to me in primary school. I studied the Roman gods; I can still name them, and I know what their various portfolios were and what their Greek counterparts were called. I can also name all of the planets, and remain fascinated by them, and the constellations. I drag my wife into the garden on frosty nights and show her where Sirius (the brightest star) is, and how to find it, hanging in line with Orion's belt.

At my primary school, we were sometimes allowed to choose and research topics. No one else did the planets, or the Roman gods, and I've no idea why I did. This was light years ago (well, several decades, anyway), but they remain on quite a short list of things I consciously remember from school, because I was allowed to follow an interest and define a way of working. There are opportunities for pupil choice in nearly every lesson (though most are less sustained than my *planets* work was). It can occur at every level of transaction. It can inform the choice of materials to work on – they choose their own sources, their own topics, their own media. They choose whether to make audio tapes or write speeches about climate change. They choose whether to write fiction or something factual about domestic life in the eighteenth century. They choose whether to be for or against the necessity of war. Of course, such choices need monitoring, and some children will tend towards easy or repetitive options, so you will need to guide them, but teachers are perfectly able to do that.

I still have a toothbrush that was given to me by a Year-8 girl years ago because I answered a question correctly about dentistry. She had given a fifteen-minute talk to the class and had chosen dentistry because it was her brother's profession. Each member of the class (they could choose to work in pairs) gave one such 'expert' talk every Friday through the year; they had a week to prepare them. One girl brought in her pony. One boy brought in his scrambler motorbike and drove it straight at us up a near-vertical bank. I was frightened at the time, but not as frightened as I am now, when I wake up in the night thinking about it. These were English lessons, but the principle of the pupil-expert, choosing, researching and presenting on subject topics can be applied anywhere in the curriculum. Are your pupils analysing their favourite music, their favourite art? Are they following individual scientific interests?

Rotation

Another simple, uncumbersome approach is that of rotation; this is also available to you without massive planning and resource creation.

A couple of years ago I had three extremely able pupils in an A-level group. They were writing essays that could have been published in academic journals, and their conversation in class was extraordinarily analytical and detailed. Of course I was aware that they shouldn't be allowed to dominate the discussion, while at the same time it was clear that less able pupils were benefiting from listening to them. Striking that balance is part of differentiation, and any decent teacher will be thinking about it. In particular, I had to be sure that the three or four pupils who were aiming at D grades didn't feel intimidated, inhibited or undervalued, and that they took part in class activities. I did this by creating discussion activities with clear structure and focus, by judicially altering groupings, by creating tasks which allowed for differentiated responses, and by generating discreetly differentiated research tasks. However, it became clear to me as I taught the class that a further group of pupils – four bright girls, who in most A-level classes would have been the predominant group – was suffering. They were interested but made little contribution to discussion, and this is vital, since moving the mouth exercises the brain; post-16 teaching is essentially discursive. These very able and conscientious pupils were being overshadowed. I decided to focus on them for about three weeks. I required their inclusion in discussion and I focused my oral and written responses on them. There was a noticeable change in their participation and confidence, though I hope and believe that no one noticed what I was doing.

At any given time, you could be focused on a given sub-group, chosen not necessarily by ability (the girls at the back, the quiet boys, the ones who don't like the topic, the middle row). Members of this group receive the bulk of your spoken and written attention for a week or two, and then you move on. It's not so defined that anyone can notice it; it doesn't exclude others; but it forces you to spread yourself evenly, and it doesn't require you to try to be all things to everyone all the time. This group, which only exists in your mind, is questioned a little more than the others; its answers are responded to a little more than the others; it works with you on guided and shared work a little more than the others; it has its written work marked a little more thoroughly than the others; and then you move on.

Multiple access: inclusion, not segregation

The principle of this chapter is that differentiation is inclusive. It works by drawing everyone from where they are towards a shared piece of learning, rather than by sending out different packets of learning to different people. Differentiated teaching provides a multiplicity of access routes. Think of the learning as a carousel;

the pupils climb on from their different points, at different speeds, in different ways. Some are quick and agile; some jump on and off as the carousel moves; some are slow and cautious, waiting for it to stop, looking for a pathway they think they can manage. Howard Gardner's concept of *Multiple Intelligences* is, at its simplest, a straightforward way of dealing with this. It has become common currency in schools, and perhaps is overdone in many, but it underlines a simple, obvious point. Different children understand things in different ways (and indeed the same child understands different things in different ways), and the implication of Gardner's list is that we should generate variety in our teaching. The original list is well-known, but I reproduce a version of it here for convenience. It is, however, possible to add to it. For example, I've found that often pupils understand new ideas when they are set into a story. You could call this *narrative intelligence*. You might like to consider what new intelligences could work well for your subject:

- *logical–mathematical intelligence*;
- *linguistic intelligence*;
- *spatial intelligence*;
- *bodily–kinaesthetic intelligence*;
- *musical intelligence*;
- *interpersonal intelligence*;
- *intrapersonal intelligence*;
- *naturalist intelligence*.

The point about multiple intelligences is not that you go into preparation overdrive creating eight or nine alternative sets of approaches and dividing the class into learning-style groups, but that you accept *one simple, basic principle* and plan that into your lessons. Consider the key, explicit learning moments; mark them on your plan; they may well occur in transitions; they will deal with the learning objectives. Decide *how you will deal with these key concepts in a variety of ways* which will create a number of access routes. All pupils can deal with all of the alternative routes; they will work differently for different individuals; they will act as reinforcements of each other for everyone.

Multiple access is a natural extension of objectives-based planning. Let's consider an example. This example is from English, but please stay with it even if it's not your subject; it applies throughout. In fact, if you haven't at this moment got a clue about iambic pentameters, my differentiated approach, set out below, should mean that, within a couple of pages, you will have, whatever your subject specialism. That's my learning objective for you. Probably, one of my routes will make the first contact, but it will be supported by some of the other approaches in building your understanding.

My objective, then, is that the pupils, who are studying Shakespeare, will understand the *iambic pentameter*. Iambic pentameter is the line structure that Shakespeare often uses in his verse. It's a ten-syllable line with alternating stress, as in, for example:

Once more unto the breach, dear friends, once more...

A good teacher will pause and explain this metrical device when she thinks it's an appropriate moment, but a brilliant teacher will decide that this is a significant piece of new learning, that it needs to become embedded and available for future use rather than being cursorily glanced at, and so that it deserves time and a range of approaches. It's a learning objective, not a note.

People will come to it in different ways and at different times. Some will hear it when you repeat a few lines of Shakespeare and point out the pattern, perhaps on the board underlining the stressed syllables, as I have above. Other people will get hold of it when they beat it out on the desk with rulers as drumsticks. Some will count it – five accents, each containing a weak and a strong beat ($5 \times 2 = 10$). Some will value the definition of the words (iamb implies 'two', pentameter means 'five', the whole means a decasyllabic line of five iambs). Some will chant it, perhaps in groups, either in words or rhythmic sounds (*ti-tum-ti-tum-ti-tum-ti-tum-ti-tum*). Some will make up their own lines (*I think I'll go and have a cup of tea...*). Some will see it when you make a diagram of it on the board:

./././././

Some will like the idea that the rhythm of iambic pentameter resembles a heartbeat. Others will want to compare it to ordinary speech, which, though obviously not as regular, has quite similar *ti-tum* stress patterns.

There are at least eight different approaches listed above, all drawn from the experience of teaching, not from a need to fulfil Gardner's list, though you will see that they do conform to several of his intelligences. These activities work together in the class-room; *there's no need to segregate them, or the pupils*; they will settle after a time on the combination that makes most sense to them. The teacher focuses on a single clear objective, rather than 'doing' the Shakespeare line-by-line; he provides a rich and varied environment for learning around a defined content focus. For each child, one or two approaches will be central, others will enrich and confirm, others will echo; the combination of analysis and creativity will generate rounded, personal understanding. *Differentiation is about synthesis and inclusion, not segregation.*

The deployment of this range of approaches is a matter of judgement; you may not use them all; you don't have to stolidly work through a sequence of activities; some of these will be brief additional suggestions. They will sometimes be a simple matter of teacher language; at other times they will involve a range of over-lapping activities. You will monitor and evaluate the learning and call up these approaches as necessary until understanding is secure. The important thing is that you've selected your key objectives and made advance planning notes about the various access possibilities. This is really common-sense teaching, but it's surprising how often teachers don't seem to have alternative routes ready in the background. If a pupil says he doesn't under-stand, how are you going to rework the learning? Far too often, teachers simply repeat and cajole, raising their voices and talking more slowly like tourists in a foreign land.

In the classroom, this will mean giving twenty minutes, not two, to the learning objective; it may mean covering less ground; it will also mean that your pupils have a chance of genuinely under-standing (and so remembering) the concept

It is true, as we said earlier, that the *multiple-intelligences/ learning-styles* movement has grabbed the attention of working teachers in a way that other (perhaps more significant) theories haven't. They certainly seem overused in teachers' language. The reduced version – VAK (visual/auditory/kinaesthetic learning) – is even more rife. It's a good thing that teachers are talking about learning, and there's no doubt that their practice has become more vital and varied as a result; but we should be careful and thought-ful about these ideas.

Kinaesthetic is a particularly well-worked analytical term. Chil-dren are asked to stand in a line, a continuum which is demon-strating something. It might be an allegiance to an idea ('Those who believe in recycling stand on the right; those who think it's a waste of time, stand on the left; now, stand in the line, depending on your attitude to recycling.'). I see this often; the children get up and decide where to stand in terms of the strength of their conviction; a jolly time is had; they sit down again. Afterwards, the teacher justifies this activity because it 'appeals to the kinaesthetic learners'.

Children for the most part like a change; they like to be able to get up and walk; they like movement. Allowing this may well engender a sense of fun and purpose in the room, and this may be adequate reason for it. But using the term *kinaesthetic* as a cover for any activity which involves practical movement may be a distraction, and it may lead the teacher into a false sense of security. Of course, kinaesthetic means, roughly, having to do with movement. But *kinaesthetic learning* is a two-word phrase, and a well-planned teacher will understand why the activity is combining the urge to move with the enhancement of the *learning*. In the case of the recycling line, the children stood at the front, looking back at their empty desks, and no doubt felt the relief we all feel when we're allowed to stretch our legs. Whether they learned anything at all about attitudes to recycling is another matter.

Perhaps they did. Perhaps they later remembered that there was a range of attitudes, with two extremes, and that they were posi-

tioned somewhere on that line. I don't know whether they did or not, because the teacher mounted the exercise so that she could show her VAK sensibility. This preoccupied her and informed this planning decision. Attaching it to recycling, and evaluating it, weren't part of the plan. She didn't pause when the line had assembled and explain to pupils what they'd done; she didn't invite pupils to look at the whole of the line and so see the continuum, the attitude-spread (and in fact it's quite hard to look at the whole of a straight line that you're also standing in). She didn't invite them to make statements about where they had chosen to stand and why; she didn't invite them to reconsider, and possibly to move up or down the line, after reflecting on other's opinions. Of course, if she had, she would have been employing auditory and visual learning as well. This would have strengthened, not weakened, the learning experience for everyone – including the 'kinaesthetics'.

All I'm saying here is that the learning is what counts. Activities must progress the learning. Of course they should be varied and address a range of learning styles; but VAK tags as justifications can never replace the centrality of the learning. With explicit planning, explanation and evaluation, there's no reason why they should, and certainly no conflict between lively activity and focused learning.

We have a chance with differentiation when we stop allowing it to be an anxious, overwhelming grind and recognise it as a spur to a lively, enjoyable, varied, inclusive and active classroom. Perhaps we need to think of it as less of a science and more of an art, at least as creative as it is analytical.

More inclusion: challenging the very able

I was watching a top-set Year-11 history class recently. The teacher (a trainee) was asking them about Mussolini; they were invited to decide whether he was a villain or, alternatively, a victim of circumstances. They were considering various evidence sources to support their judgements. The lesson moved to a whole-class feedback discussion around this question.

I have watched this process often; I've done it myself many times. The teacher takes points on both sides of the discussion. There is an element of creative competition between the two viewpoints and the evidence is being well-adduced from the readings.

This is going well; but these are very clever children. Inevitably, at some point, one of them says, 'Well, I think he's both.'

The very able often show themselves in this way, by seeming to opt out of the teacher's structures. The two or three pupils who refuse to play *victim or villain* are probably not intending to be difficult. What they are doing is signalling to the teacher that he needs to raise his game; the discussion needs to move to a more sophisticated level. In real life, no one is entirely victim or villain; even a dictator is in reality a complex mixture, and these able children have seen that and want to talk about it. This is a wonderful moment in your teaching, reflecting real and subtle engagement from your pupils. How are you to make the best of such an opportunity?

A good teacher will be listening for this and not limited by his own agenda. Such a departure is a movement upwards in terms of thinking skills. He will focus on it and invite further explanation and analysis. He will probably invite the whole class to consider this new perception.

These are some of the ways in which we cater for gifted and talented children. We listen carefully to them. We allow them to extend the learning structures, to push at the concepts. We also encourage them to synthesise and compare.

A creative aspect of this challenge lies in synthesis. Able children are able (and must be encouraged) to make connections; teaching has to move from initial materials into wider contexts. Pupils may come to a preliminary understanding that Mussolini is neither victim nor villain, but these concepts are only fully understood when they are extrapolated. Tell the pupils to find other examples of the *victim/villain* dichotomy – in fiction, in drama, in *Eastenders*, in politics, in the newspapers, in society, away from the lesson, at home, away from the war, away from school. They could research this material for homework and discuss it in class. The single *victim/villain* objective is now being rehearsed into a wide range of contexts. The concept is being roundly explored and fully understood. It is being abstracted.

To take another example: consider very able pupils understanding the mathematical concept of symmetry from the original lesson outlined in Chapter 5. Imagine some of these pupils now carrying that single objective into new contexts. From the clarity and focus of that initial, graphical discovery (a whiteboard diagram), they can now find symmetry in paintings, in poetry, in science, in snowflakes, in arguments, in political debate, in music. Imagine a Year-8 pupil able to comment that a particular story or argument isn't very symmetrical. What he has been able to do is to transfer a concept from its origin to a range of new environments. No process better indicates sophisticated and confident understanding.

Differentiation: from C to A

In particular, this able child has been encouraged to move from the *concrete* to the *abstract*. This is a movement that helps us to define and conceive teaching and learning that is inclusive and differentiated. We talked about this relationship in Chapter 5. I recently watched some Year-10 pupils analysing holiday brochures in a Business Studies lesson. They were being asked to consider potential audiences for these brochures which are, of course, essentially advertisements. Quite properly, the teacher had asked them to compare two brochures featuring holidays clearly intended for different markets, remembering that comparing two things is always more than twice as effective as analysing one.

This was a mixed-ability option group and there was a wide range of conversations, which the teacher was managing and prompting very effectively. It occurred to me as I watched that differentiation in the room was happening not via stepped worksheets but by the teacher's language. In particular, he consistently moved between the concrete and the abstract.

We might consider here some of the topics he covered and the questions he asked (Table 6.1).

This was a skilled and experienced teacher; he was deploying these concrete and abstract questions instinctively, moving (apparently seamlessly) between them, not obviously demarking different groups within the room, working with the whole group towards a shared understanding. You will see that he invited concrete thinkers and abstract thinkers to cover similar ground, but that the concrete thinkers focused on themselves, their opinions, experiences and reactions, whereas the abstract thinkers were required to be more formally, explicitly and technically analytical of how the brochures worked. The concrete thinkers consider the *what* of the question; the abstract thinkers explore the *how* and the *why*.

Table 6.1 From concrete to abstract

high

ABSTRACT

explicit	analytical	formal	how and why

> ### HOLIDAY BROCHURE ANALYSIS
>
> What is the primary function?
> How does the tone support this function? (e.g. reassurance, excitement)
> How is the tone achieved? (e.g. verb person, sentence lengths)
> What techniques are used particularly to sell the holiday?
> What is the target audience for the advert?
> What other audiences are there?
> Comment on the use of specialist vocabulary.
> In what ways are the text and pictures related in terms of the tone and purpose of the brochure?
> Can you see examples of exaggeration or euphemism?
>
>
> What is the primary function?
> Does it work on you?
> What's your idea of a perfect holiday?
> Which of the two holidays would you choose?
> Why would you choose that one?
> What could be wrong with the holiday?
> Have you been on a holiday that wasn't at all like the brochure promised?
> Describe a typical day on the brochure holiday.
> Which of the holidays do you think would be the more friendly?
> Which of the two holidays is for older people or families?

implicit	descriptive	personal	what

CONCRETE

low

In planning, therefore, you could be asking yourself:

- Have I got enough concrete questions to support the less able learners?
- Have I got enough abstract questions to challenge the more able learners?

Considering these two questions may lead you to make a few additions to your lesson plan and to (therefore) offer a broader range of opportunities in the classroom. When you start to do this, you are making serious inroads into differentiation.

Meta-learning

In discussing differentiation, we are considering axes along which we can map thinking and learning skills. We have just considered that one fruitful axis runs from concrete to abstract. In fact, any decent lesson could run in that direction; concepts are approached concretely, via example (such as a symmetry diagram on the board); then they are enlarged and abstracted. The more able can pursue the abstraction more fully, generalising the concepts into new contexts and understandings. Another set of higher-order skills concerns how fully children can understand and shape their own learning.

Talented pupils can be extended when teachers allow them access to the learning process. This can be very exciting to watch, and here are some examples of how teachers do it. I have seen all of these from time to time and, in every case, they have pushed the learning beyond the banal.

Instead of publishing the learning objectives on the board at the start of the lesson, they might conduct the lesson and then, at the end, ask the pupils what the objectives were. In fact, they are inviting the pupils to deconstruct or reverse-engineer the lesson; to work out (perhaps in a plenary pair discussion) why they have been doing what they've been doing; to connect the lesson activities and stages, to see what the running story or theme of the lesson has been. This requires an active and analytical understanding of the learning and high-level synthesis.

Instead of presenting the objectives and then setting out the activities, they might inform the pupils of the objectives and then ask them to plan the activities which will be most appropriate. In Chapter 3, I described doing precisely this with a speech-marks English lesson. The children share in the lesson planning.

When setting up the main (centre) lesson activity, they might ask pupils to decide on the connection of this to the just-completed starter activity. They are inviting pupils to see the lesson journey and perhaps to script the transition, providing the words which the teacher could use to draw out the learning objective from the first activity and transfer it to the next. You might just say, from time to time, 'What's this got to do with what we were doing before?'.

They might invite pupils to predict aspects of the lesson. One of the most powerful (but least used) teacher questions is 'What do you think I'm going to say next?'. The most able may be able to predict your thinking; they may see the direction of the learning. Apart from involving pupils, this is an effective form of evaluation. Consider the analytical power of a teacher question like, 'What do you think I'm going to ask you about this?'

For example, a teacher shows children a painting.

- A *competent* teacher may tell them about the painting.
- A *good* teacher may ask them questions about the painting.
- A *brilliant* teacher may ask them what questions they anticipate being asked about the painting, or what questions they themselves would ask about it.

The third variant is brilliant because it requires the children to frame the analysis. It requires them to think not just about the painting but about the whole process of talking about paintings, and this is much more significant to the learning than the painting itself.

Stepping back: naive sophistication

This idea was crystallised for me when I saw the same question asked twice in one week. I was watching English lessons, and the teachers, in both cases, were working on *themes*. Themes are an important part of the study of a novel or a play, and no doubt you remember them from your own schooldays; however, they aren't important to us now, except as an example. In both of these lessons, the teacher was introducing the themes of a novel – a very common thing to do in an English lesson. She was talking, questioning and listing possible themes on the whiteboard. The unexpected question which was asked by a pupil in each lesson was not a question you hear very often. It was, 'What *is* a theme?'.

A question like that brings you to a halt. It's so obvious that you have never thought of it. I remembered all the time I'd taught about themes, all the times I'd marked examination papers about themes. I had never discussed what themes are, or why they matter. I had discussed the question 'What are *the* themes?' ad nauseam. I had never once addressed the entirely different question 'What *are* themes?'.

But what struck me most was the two contexts in which this same question was asked. On the first occasion, it was asked by a child with special educational needs. The second questioner was a high-flying Year-10 pupil obviously already capable of an A* and all that came after it. For a few moments, that week, their needs were identical. They needed the teacher to stop making assumptions. They needed explicitness and definition. They needed the teacher to step back from the programme and to take a longer view of it.

The answers given were broadly similar also, at least to begin with. The subsequent conversations diverged, obviously; the pupil with SEN was now able to begin looking for themes, knowing what he was looking for; the bright Year-10 pupil was able to talk about the fundamentals of themes, to consider them in the abstract for the first time, to analyse the notion of theme and where it fitted into the broader study. In both cases, the teachers needed to move from the middle ground, the comfortable area of unspoken assumptions, and to look afresh at the fundamentals. In tracking back to those basics, the teachers met needs across the whole ability spectrum; they met the needs of concrete and abstract learners. A scientist describing the annual conference of the American Association for the Advancement of Science recently remarked, 'The most challenging questions being asked by scientists now – *Who are we? What are we made of? Why are we here?* – are the questions asked by small children.' The middle-ground teacher (see Chapter 5) talks about types of maps, types of experiments, different sorts of equations; but the dynamic teacher asks 'What *are* maps? What *is* an experiment?'. They're challenging questions with fascinating, broad-ranging and inclusive answers.

For example: what is a *map*? We may teach about different sorts of maps, but we may consider that defining a map itself is a basic question – an early-years question, or a primary question. In fact, of course, it's potentially a very sophisticated question indeed. It's also quite cross-curricular. In fact, in some ways, it's a question that goes to the heart of what a classroom does.

A map represents. The many ways in which it can do this are fascinating, but at its heart it's a microcosm. The idea of what's outside, everywhere, being reduced to a small piece of paper is extraordinary. In this sense, a map resembles a scientific experiment. The real world is caught and reduced, so that we can look at it. A metaphor or a sonnet does the same thing. So does a textbook. The potential for sophisticated cross-curricular understanding is considerable here, as we look at all the codes, systems and tricks that we use to get control of the universe. Which, of course, is what teachers are trying to do, every day, in the classroom.

Chapter 7

Evaluation

Evaluation is perhaps the most potent engine of your development as a teacher. In one sense, it's happening all the time. Almost everything that happens to you in school – every question asked, every corridor conversation, every book marked – is evaluative of your work. This is relentless, and, if you think about it too much, it's also potentially terrifying. On the other hand, you can't afford to ignore it if you want to improve. So what matters most about evaluation is, as ever, that you make it work for you. It must be your servant, and not vice versa. For this to happen, you have to develop a rational and serviceable evaluative practice.

Assessment and evaluation are related, but they aren't the same thing. We will talk about assessment in the next chapter, but for now it concerns us only in that it provides evaluative input. *Assessment is what we do to children's work; evaluation is what we do to our own.* It's helpful to keep this in mind, and to consciously disentangle these two activities. They are easily confused. They bear on each other, they look like each other, they use similar language, they use some of the same data, and they often happen at the same time. When you evaluate in a plenary, for example, you are certainly evaluating the children's learning; but you are also evaluating your own teaching. In your reflection (see next chapter) you have to explicitly separate out this self-evaluation to make sense of your own development.

You may already be involved in evaluative systems. Schools often run appraisal or review schemes which may include self-review or peer-review of your teaching. If you are concerned to develop your career, you may need to move beyond these schemes, using their findings perhaps as starting points for your own sustained self-evaluation. If you don't have ambitious career plans but just want to be a decent teacher (a very commendable place to be, in my opinion), you still probably need to expand any review system that you're part of – if only because, by so doing, you are making it your own. Such schemes can be quite limited, anyway. Peer-observation systems, for example, often only focus on teaching, whereas you might benefit greatly from work on your performance in meetings, in assessment, in parents' evenings.

The most complex and potentially useful school schemes almost always centre on appraisal or review systems. In many cases, a wide range of information may be collected about you and shared with you. The best appraisals, of course, aren't top-down, oppressive affairs; they are collaborative, and appraisee-driven. I remember introducing appraisal into a school in the very early days of these schemes. It was met with frank hostility by the staff, especially as it was widely believed (and originally intended) to be linked to salary. That was when I first heard the maxim, 'Appraisal is not part of the problem; it's part of the solution.' This formula, since applied widely and mendaciously to anything threatening, has become a cliché; but I still think it's a useful test. In that school, the change in attitude to appraisal was remarkable, as people realised that, when properly constituted, it gave them a voice that they hadn't had before. Any evaluation system should support you in school, even if it's one you've invented yourself. But much more importantly, it should help you to be a better teacher.

Lesson evaluation

For me, evaluating lessons used to be a subjective business. As the children left the room, I would say, 'Well, I think that went rather well!' or, 'Well, they seemed to enjoy it...'. If I had taught something, quite well in my opinion, to an apparently interested class, then my assumption was that they had learned it. This is still a common equation: *decent teaching plus reasonably co-operative class equals learning.* When asking a question such as, 'Why are you sure they all understand congruent triangles?' I frequently receive the answer, 'Because we did them last week.'

But I did used to notice discontinuities – for example, the disappointing discrepancy between what seemed to be a lively lesson and a poor written follow-up. Concepts were explained, discussed and illuminated in the lesson, perhaps largely orally (and perhaps with excess YAVA); but later in the week, when I read the resulting

writing, I would be surprised to find that understanding was far from secure. This has happened to me many times. I am swayed by an active and cheerful speaking-and-listening session into a subjective, implicit but wayward evaluation of the learning, and this is only corrected days later. Of course, your impression of the lesson is important, but your evaluation can't stop there. Evaluation needs to be swifter, more objective and more explicit than that.

You need to evaluate your own work for two essential and connected purposes: to improve pupil learning and to improve your own practice. If pupils aren't learning, you need to consider very quickly how to modify your approaches. When things go well, you need to clarify the success for yourself so that you can build on it both in terms of their immediate learning and your continuing development.

Brilliant teachers are evaluating pretty well all of the time, and this may seem a daunting prospect. However, it's possible to rationalise evaluation into a straightforward and highly manageable component of lesson planning.

What evaluation isn't

Let's continue to clarify what good evaluation isn't. We've said that it shouldn't be purely impressionistic. Neither is evaluation an afterthought; it is *an essential component of your planning, built into your lesson before you teach it.* This may be one of the biggest attitude shifts that we, as experienced and busy teachers, need to manage as we build an evaluative process. The word itself suggests something that happens afterwards. But this isn't accurate. For one thing, evaluation is a constant part of life. At this moment, somewhere within you (explicitly or implicitly), you're evaluating this book and deciding if it's worth spending any more time on. So evaluation is available throughout the lesson, not just at the end. And for another thing, while you can't conduct post-lesson evaluation before the lesson (obviously), you can and should *plan* it.

However, for reasons of practical and emotional sanity, evaluation can't be a complete sweep of everything that happens. It needs to be focused. If allowed to run out of control, it attempts to cover everything – the children's entry into the room, how quickly they settled, whether the weather affected them, whether it was Friday afternoon, how well they responded to questioning, whether they were silent when asked, how much help they needed with the tasks, how noisy they were, whether you talked too much, how well you explained things, how your pace and timing went, how effectively you prepared and used resources... The problem with such diffuse and ambitious evaluation is that it can obscure the only question that really matters. *Did they achieve the learning objectives?* All other questions are subsidiaries.

The information that marking and assessment provide naturally helps us to evaluate the effectiveness of our teaching; but it can be a cumbersome process and we need to evaluate on a short timescale as well. We need to plan the next lesson, or the next stage of the lesson, or the next sentence of our explanation, in the light of how things are going. At least, we need to evaluate the learning before the lesson ends, so that we can modify our plans for tomorrow.

What evaluation is

At its simplest, evaluation is asking and answering three questions as your pupils leave the classroom:

* *What were they meant to learn?*
* *Did they learn it?*
* *How do I know?*

Earlier chapters on the centrality of learning objectives (especially Chapters 2 and 3) dealt with the first of these; and one of the advantages of working always to clear and specific objectives is that you have a basis for answering the other two questions, and this is your basis for evaluation.

Three levels of evaluation

It helps to think of evaluation as happening at three levels. At a minimum level, you need to evaluate learning at the end of each lesson. At another level, it is a permanent feature of your teaching. There is a middle way between these which is highly effective and might be a good place to begin creating a semi-formal evaluation practice.

The middle level: evaluating activities

As we have said repeatedly, the lesson has a progressive narrative – a story. The first activity creates a piece of understanding which, at the transition point, will be discussed explicitly and then developed into a second activity. The transition point, as we've said, is a crucial learning moment. It's also a crucial moment of evaluation.

So you might establish a habit of evaluating learning at each transition point – after each activity. I recently watched a lesson with a middle-ability Year-10 group which was about pre-twentieth-century short stories (a common GCSE component and a familiar interpretation of Key-Stage-4 requirements). The teacher wanted to explain that stories reflect the culture in which they're written. She began by explaining what she meant by culture – listening to this was the pupils' first activity. They were then given statements about nineteenth-century culture which they had to match against the plots of three or four stories, which they'd previously read.

This matching exercise was well-prepared and potentially very effective, but the pupils struggled with it. It became clear that many of them were confused by the initial definition of culture which was essential for the second activity to work. *The first activity (pupil listening) had not been evaluated – their understanding had not been checked and was in fact far short of the teacher's assumptions.* Had the first activity been more interactive, evaluation would have presented itself by default; however, in the event, the teacher needed to be sure that the pupils understood, but had planned no method of finding out. A potentially excellent and well-planned lesson failed because of this.

I see this often. The lesson is well-crafted. The activities fit together and the lesson story is obvious in the plan. The first activity delivers a piece of learning which will be taken further in the next activity.

Or rather, it doesn't. It does on the plan. It does in the teacher's head. But when that first activity closes, the teacher has no idea of its effectiveness. Significant numbers haven't got it, and they begin to drift because they can't make sense of the next activity. The teacher doesn't know this; she becomes concerned with behaviour management; her post-lesson analysis is about rewards and sanctions, teacher authority, and so on. She can't see what went wrong and so she can't put it right.

Our structure should be based on explicit evaluation at the end of each activity. We need to know now whether the pupils have any sense of what we mean by culture, or euphemism, or attrition, or symmetry. We can't go on to our next activity without being sure of this, and we can't just assume that they've learned it because we've taught it.

How does activity-level evaluation happen?

For this straightforward system of evaluating each activity, we need to plan the evaluative mechanism; this is part of your lesson plan, which now has *evaluation* as a standard component.

So you clarify in your plan the closing activity which will evaluate the learning. This will be a brief activity, joined more or less seamlessly to the learning activity, or integrated within it. It will be a significant part of the transition. As well as providing you with a snapshot of the learning up to that point, it will enable the pupils to sustain and consolidate that learning for themselves. Of course, the simplest method is to ask children if they understand, but this has limited value. Children usually say they understand, even when they don't; they frankly prefer bewilderment to a repetition of the explanation. (This reminds me of asking for directions when lost in the car. A helpful local gives accurate but complicated directions through the window. I don't follow a word of it, but I always pretend I do. Why do we do this?) So try some slightly more elaborate methods:

- They could discuss in pairs a key question about the learning, and then feed back their answers.
- They could give their own created examples – for example, their own euphemisms or their own riddles.
- They could create a one-sentence explanation for other pupils in other classes.
- They could write three key words on their whiteboards.
- They could design their own evaluative questions.
- They could restate the learning objectives in new words.
- They could suggest what the next objective might be.
- They could provide a real-world example of dramatic irony.
- They could explain how this activity related to earlier ones in previous lessons.

Permanent evaluation

You are probably doing a good deal of this already. It doesn't replace the need for more formal evaluation after each activity or, at least, at the end of each lesson. It does require you to be highly sensitive as you monitor reactions in the room.

Almost any classroom activity provides evaluative information and brilliant teachers are permanently susceptible to this. From the first moment of any lesson, you are bombarded with evaluative input. This isn't especially scientific or even systematic – for example, it doesn't always evaluate the learning of every individual – but it's immensely valuable in steering the work. When children are reading aloud, you are checking whether they understand what they're reading and reflecting on the appropriateness of the text. When you question the class, you have immediate insight from the nature and frequency of their answers into the appropriateness of the level of work and your explanations so far. Their questions to you signal their comfort level. For example, when you set a task and ask for questions (QDO) and you are faced with a large number of them, you know immediately that your explanation has been unclear and you should stop and re-present it to the whole group. When they're discussing in pairs, you are listening to snippets of discussion; when they're writing, you're looking over their shoulders. When they're feeding back, you're checking their understanding; when they're collaborating with you in a piece of shared writing, you're aware of whether they get the points

about the nature of what you're doing. When you're talking to the whole class, you're looking at their faces. The more interactive your teaching becomes, the more frequent and immediate is the evaluation. Literacy Framework starters, for example, model teaching which provides evaluative data minute-by-minute. You aren't just estimating whether they're getting it right; you're estimating whether the teaching is doing its job, is accurately pitched and effectively carried out.

The plenary for end-of-lesson evaluation

The UK Secondary Strategy recognises the value of a final lesson activity which consolidates and evaluates the learning. This is a highly significant and effective component of the three-part lesson, though it is often neglected. Books of starters have been published, but the plenary suffers by comparison. Because of problems with timing, and perhaps a general feeling that there isn't much point to it, the plenary quite often disappears in practice; or it is relegated to setting homework and packing up or to a quick 'What did we learn today?' session, on the bell, the pupils already standing up to leave. At this point, they'll say anything to get out of the room. If the objectives are obvious to them, they'll say they understand them. This is quite possibly meaningless.

Your hour lesson needs a ten-minute plenary (not a five-minute one), and this needs to be a planned activity which will enable you to gauge the mood of the room in terms of your learning objectives, to have a sense at least of the majority achievement, and to consider modifications for tomorrow. Routine is good here, but so is variety; so your plenary activity could be chosen from a list such as this:

- I didn't tell you today's objectives – now, what do you think they were?
- Explain today's learning in one sentence to a specified audience such as your Mum, a seven-year-old child, a class in the year below yours.
- In pairs – what was the most important thing *in your opinion* that you learned today?
- Sum up today's learning in exactly fifteen words.
- In pairs, think up a new (better?) activity to teach today's objective.
- Write an advertisement or a film trailer for today's lesson.
- Write a two-minute radio news story summing up what happened in today's lesson.
- That's the objective – but tell me one other thing you learned today.
- Look back at today's activities – what was the connection?
- Write a newspaper headline for today's lesson.
- Write one more example of your own.
- As a class, complete two columns on the whiteboard headed CLEAR and NOT CLEAR (or GOT? and NOT GOT?) about what we've learned and what still confuses us.
- One thing from today that needs more explanation.
- What do you guess next lesson will be about, and why?
- What does next lesson *need* to be about?

Even suggestions beginning *Write* here are predominantly speaking and listening suggestions. You will emphasise speed here; you will glance at the jottings; you will listen to as many contributions as possible – evaluative plenaries are swift and interactive.

Some of the later suggestions on this list suggest how a sustained habit of evaluation through plenaries and elsewhere can generate a truly collaborative classroom ethos. Pupils are being invited to drive the learning forward explicitly by considering where it needs to go next. They are participating in evaluation not so much of their own work or of the teacher's efforts but of the learning as a joint operation. The following lesson can in a sense be jointly planned, or at least modified. The teacher can offer her proposed alternatives for tomorrow's lesson and invite comment. The responsibility for the learning is being shared.

This doesn't mean, obviously, that the final responsibility isn't yours. If learning isn't secure, or behaviour is not as it should be, you have to consider what you can do about your own practice to improve things rather than simply blaming children for misbehaving or not listening carefully. Evaluation should provoke two levels of activity for you. In the short (or immediate) term, it might lead you to change the work currently under way with a specific class. In the longer term, it should help you with forward planning and your own development. Table 7.1 shows some judgements and consequent actions which I noted training teachers taking over a period of a few weeks. Experienced teachers may feel that they don't need to be as explicit; but reaction notes

Table 7.1 Evaluation and action

Input	Evaluation	Short-term action	Long-term action
Children reading Shakespeare aloud badly – stumbling, etc.	Text more challenging than I'd thought; lower understanding than anticipated	More text editing, more active approaches, more checking of learning	More care over text choices; more forward planning re: editing; more DARTs; more checking of understanding
Nearly half the class had questions after task-setting	Explanation not as detailed as it needed to be; no QDO	Stopped class, went through instructions more carefully; QDO	Plan instructions, task-setting more elaborately; anticipate pupil problems; test instructions on spouse; write out instruction script for self
Disappointing feedbacks after good group discussions	Not enough time and structure given specifically for the feedbacks	Stopped after two feedbacks and encouraged all groups to spend ten more minutes on them	Vary feedbacks; sometimes, no feedback at all; treat feedback as separate task needing its own structure and time
Children inattentive during reading of textbook	Children were bored by text. Text is inaccessible for some	Stopped reading after fifteen minutes	Think carefully about choice of texts; vary reading strategies and voices; use shorter reading periods; give focus questions before the reading; QDO (especially O) before reading
Plenary revealed continuing confusion between congruent and similar triangles	Probably compounded confusion by teaching the two together	Stopped lesson and redefined	Don't teach pairs like this! It just seals in the confusion. Teach one or the other in its own context

like these would help you to arrange your thoughts and focus on the two complementary but not identical purposes of evaluation – improvement for the children, improvement for you.

In these cases we see teachers using various levels of input to evaluate their work, making immediate modification if necessary and then considering their own development. While written outcomes certainly provide rich evaluative material, the more immediate evaluations happen in active and interactive lessons. The more pupil involvement, the more obvious the evaluation. This can be formalised into whole systems of pupil evaluation, where pupils evaluate each other's work and their own. Pupils certainly benefit from systematic evaluation of their own work and brilliant teachers invite this through regular discussion and by encouraging pupils to reflect, perhaps in writing, as a matter of course. Pupil logs can contain progressive personal accounts of developments, problems solved, talents fostered, preferences discovered. As well as benefiting pupils, such logs support teachers in the continuing task of evaluating and improving their own work.

Chapter 8

Moving on

There are many ways of developing your career. Indeed, this whole business now has its own set of initials (CPD) and there are many formal programmes within schools, local authorities and universities. Increasingly, teachers at all stages of their careers are encouraged to obtain higher-degree qualifications of the sort that would have been considered exotic when I began teaching. Many PGCE students in the UK are now being offered master's-level credits alongside their initial training, so that they enter the profession with part (or sometimes all) of a master's degree; and these qualifications are certainly career-enhancing. This is a book about teaching and learning rather than about career structures and, in reaching some conclusions about moving on and getting better, it is to teaching and learning that I want to return. Nevertheless, it's appropriate to look first (and briefly) at some formal aspects of continued professional development.

Teacher-learner

If you're fairly new in your career, a lot of this will look (perhaps depressingly) familiar. If you're some years in, you will notice that we are considering switching you into a new mode – a new way of thinking about your job. We mentioned this switch in Chapter 1; you may have to make it now if you want to move on. It can feel almost retrogressive; it may seem that you're being asked to revisit a sort of student-teacher mode that you thought you'd left behind. You can function perfectly well without portfolios, evaluations and evidence. Possibly, you can function well enough without lesson plans. But you need to step back if you want to move forward.

The main point about this switch is that you once again make your practice explicit, so that you can look straight at it and improve it. Student teachers have no choice about this; they can only learn to teach through explicitness, and implicitness only comes with experience. But for you to move back into explicitness may at first feel artificial. It's vital, because it's a move away from the sort of skilled pragmatism with which most teachers (inevitably) operate. It's true that to do this you may have to do some things that you associate with your initial training – researching, gathering evidence, evaluating, reading theory. But in truth it's not a backward step. Perhaps we need to invent a new term for this kind of teacher – not *student-teacher*, but *teacher-student*, *teacher-learner*, or *teacher-researcher*.

You may want to begin to build your career prospects by undertaking formal CPD and, obviously, you will make enquiries in school, with your Local Authority and any local training providers to see what sort of modules might be available. These will often be *postgraduate certificates* which will provide credits at master's level. Undertaking any extra work is a serious business for a schoolteacher, and one important criterion in making any such choice should be that it has minimum negative impact on your professional (and personal) life. So it's a good idea to look for courses that work through group sessions within your own school. Some sort of *school improvement* module, for example, is likely to attract colleagues from other departments, and this will provide a local support system. You may well be able to work with school colleagues in terms of research. Similarly, you should seek modules which take account of the work you are already doing. You may be working as a *subject leader*, or as a training *mentor*, and often such work, presented in terms of written reflection and analysis, will contribute directly to your CPD. For example, if you are a newly qualified teacher, you can probably take modules in *teaching and learning* which will, in effect, credit the work you need to do in your induction year. In all cases, I'm suggesting that you keep the CPD as close to home as possible. You are busy enough as it is.

Keeping a portfolio

Much of this sort of work centres on reflection and evaluation. This will manifest in discussion and of course in writing. If your initial training was in the last decade you are probably familiar with the business of keeping a portfolio of evidence and reflection. As an NQT you will be delighted to discover that you have to continue to do this; and, indeed, this is becoming common at many levels of the profession. Maintaining a portfolio is, therefore, a good habit to get into. It will support your formal career development but (more importantly) it will also help you to reflect on your work and to become a better teacher.

The contents of a portfolio may well be dictated by any CPD or in-house evaluation scheme in which you are involved. As well as postgraduate modules connected with external CPD, such as those mentioned above, you might be maintaining an evidence file in connection with your career path through your school. This may consist of evidencing that you've met certain Standards relating to the career stage that you've reached or aspire to. In the UK currently there are Standards for:

- Qualified Teacher Status (Q);
- Guidance for Newly Qualified Teachers;
- Mainscale Teachers (C);
- Upper Payscale ('Post-Threshold') Teachers (P);
- Excellent Teachers (E);
- Advanced Skills Teachers (A).

A good starting point, then, might be to set yourself targets of evidence gathering around appropriate Standards.

A portfolio will often have two main components. It will show evidence that Standards have been met; and it will carry reflective writing.

Let's first consider *evidence*. Evidence is easy to gather. It will include:

- lesson plans;
- schemes of work;
- samples of pupil response – written work;
- samples of marked pupil work;
- your own evaluations of your own (and other colleagues') lessons;
- colleagues' evaluations of your teaching;
- evidence of INSET;
- evidence of effective pastoral work;

- evidence of effective professional work (meeting agendas and minutes, for example);
- formal evidence of pupil achievement (examination results);

and so on. The list is bordering on the infinite, so before you begin to gather evidence you should decide what your portfolio is for, and what evidence is essential for that. If you're only maintaining a portfolio for your personal development as a teacher (rather than for a specified career intention) then you should probably focus on evidence of growth in teaching and learning.

One problem with such portfolios is that they can become very large and unfocused. Good portfolio evidence is clearly targeted, and its relevance is explained in the writing which accompanies it. A further, effective focusing method is the compiling of composite evidence. A scheme of work may be associated with a lesson plan, a pupil outcome, and an evaluation, so that the portfolio becomes holistic in character rather than atomistic. Similarly, a portfolio can show progress using a set of evidence relating to a specific development. A lesson plan, an evaluation, a piece of research and another, later lesson plan (which shows progress from the earlier plan; you reflected and learned something new) together demonstrate an improving practice. Your portfolio should tell a story.

The other part of your portfolio is the *reflective writing* which comments on your development and your evidence of it. Remember that, whatever the ostensible or external audience and purpose for this writing, in terms of specific courses or qualifications, you've only really got time for it (and it will only become truly effective) if it helps you to understand your achievements and to have new thoughts about them. In your busy life as a teacher, reflection should be a moment's peace.

It may be some time since you did reflective writing; some people are quite alarmed by the prospect. One of the main issues here is that of confidence. Some teachers suspect that reflective writing has a particular set of formal requirements which they haven't met before, or have forgotten. But this isn't true; there are some conventions which allow reflective writing to happen, but they are based on common sense, and are fairly flexible. You may in the past have been confronted with quite specific formal requirements ('Never write in the first person!') for academic writing, but the expectations around reflective writing are much more diverse and relaxed. It is, after all, essentially personal. *If*

you can think about what's happening to you, and try to under-
stand why and what to do about it, you can do reflective writing.

Let's consider the content of reflective writing. Its purpose, as
we've said, is to examine experiences and draw conclusions. The
experiences in question are varied. You may, for example, reflect
on lessons. You may reflect on conversations, reading, your own
planning, other people's planning, meetings or training events.
Just about everything that happens to you provides some food for
thought.

Naturally, this richness makes it necessary to make some
choices. One way of doing this is to consider your own specific
career path and intentions. You might want to select events which
have impacted on a chosen focus. You found it hard to motivate
disaffected children, but you have made progress in this area. Or
you have done excellent work in developing your subject knowledge. So now you have to make a list of the experiences which
contributed to this development, or which specifically evidence
this achievement. Alternatively, perhaps there have been some

memorable, critical moments in your work – moments when things moved on, when corners were turned. These could be key lessons, key conversations, key readings – critical events which you could use as the focus for your writing.

Reflective writing, then, is personal and may even be anecdotal up to a point, but this doesn't mean that it's not rigorous. In particular, it needs to be analytical. The line between description and analysis troubles some people, but it's not really difficult. *Writing becomes analytical when it asks the question 'Why?'*. It's also precisely at this point that it becomes useful to you.

Consider this example.

> I wanted to begin with a recap of the previous lesson using pair discussion. There were some discussion prompts and questions on the desks to get them started. However they didn't settle very well, and one boy was so disruptive that I had to send him out. They didn't really answer the questions and in the end I had to quieten the class and remind them what had happened in the previous lesson as well as telling them that I wasn't very pleased with their attitude. They did finally settle down to the main task, which was reading and understanding a source text, and then the lesson went quite well.

This is a genuine and sincere (and early) attempt at reflective writing and it clearly shows a teacher trying to think about her experiences. It's not a bad starting point, but it is descriptive rather than analytical. You might try counting the number of times this piece skates over the question *why?*. I think it does so eight or nine times. Try a similar count on your own writing if people are telling you that you need to be more analytical. Why did she want a recap? Why did she want it to be in pairs? Why were there written discussion prompts? Why did the pupils not settle? You may not need to answer every question, but dealing with some or most of them will produce a far more mature and considered piece:

> I think that a recap is always essential. Children have had many school and non-school experiences since last lesson and need to refocus to establish continuity. On this occasion I wanted to use pair discussion to involve all of them in doing

more than just listening to me and to give them a chance to support each other. I decided to place written prompts on the desks so that they could get started immediately, without the need to listen to me at all, and so that they knew exactly what to focus on. However, the recap didn't really succeed, and, on reflection, I think that the class needed a brief spoken comment from me to create a more definite beginning to the lesson. Listening to them later, it also became clear to me that the prompts I'd given them were too challenging and they had been unable to work with them without help.

It's obvious how much stronger the second piece is; real reflection is now beginning. You'll notice that there is analysis of both expected and unexpected events. You can always offer ready explanations of why you did certain things – after all, you had your reasons. But you also have to reflect on outcomes. This is less immediate, but in this case she comes up with some possible explanations (and she omits the purely anecdotal incident of the naughty boy).

Reconnecting with theory

The second piece above is beginning to be analytical, but it's hardly master's-level reflection. It needs to be further supported, perhaps by references to learning theory, which might help you to understand and diagnose more fully. It's likely, however, that you haven't read much learning theory for a long time. Indeed, you may be about to skip this section altogether. Theory is another thing we don't have time to do, feel slightly guilty about, and (therefore) reject with a kind of bravado – 'I can manage perfectly well without that!'.

It may be true – up to a point. I don't believe I read a word of learning theory during my training or my first twenty years as a teacher. The suggestion that I should spend my spare time reading it (and indeed, the suggestion that I had any spare time) would be met with a hollow laugh. But I did have the slightly less typical experience of transferring to teacher training later on. At this point I had to read a range of theory, and I found it revealing. It told me new things; it told me new ways of thinking about old things; and it told me that I'd been doing constructivist teaching all my life. I was theoretically kosher, without knowing it. This feeling of smug discovery gave way, however, to a sense of chagrin. It took me years of trial and error to sort out my thinking about how to be a teacher. If someone had shown me Bruner and Vygotsky, I could have saved a lot of time and effort.

Theory is there; it reflects the work of people who have spent their lives considering how children learn things; you can't seriously ignore it any more than a surgeon can ignore anatomy. But there's a lot of it, you have no time for it, and it doesn't look particularly attractive. What are you supposed to do?

For a start, you could spend a little time developing *your own theories of learning*. You are an experienced teacher. You have had successes and failures. Because you work (as we've said) at the level of skilled pragmatism, your consideration of your own classroom may be limited to practical problem solving; and you're probably very good at that. But in developing a truly evaluative practice (see Chapter 7) and coupling it with a more sustained approach to reflection, you become able to develop your own theories of learning. Doing that first might help you to approach and appreciate other people's.

We talked in the previous chapter about evaluation. If you want to develop seriously career-promoting reflective practice, you may need to move evaluation beyond the tripartite lesson-evaluation system set out there. Later we will touch on how teachers research; but one way to move towards being a teacher-researcher is to mount sustained and deep evaluation of your own teaching. Why not develop evaluative mechanisms for many or all your lessons? You can create written feedback sheets which pupils may complete every lesson, or once a week. This is not a common practice, and that isn't surprising. If your pupils are anonymous and honest, you may sometimes find their comments dispiriting. At times, of course, they will misrepresent their own feelings. But nevertheless, a systematic flow of commentary from pupils about their learning in your lessons would be enormously helpful as a basis for reflection and improvement.

The benefits of such practice would be substantial; but nevertheless, it sounds like a formidable programme. How could you make it practicable? You could work through samples. Use some (not all) of your classes, and sample randomly within them – perhaps three or four pupils each time. Design a feedback sheet which mixes straightforward countable answers ('Did you successfully achieve the learning objectives?') with space for brief prose responses ('How could I have better explained it?'). When you collate this, you will not produce dazzling rows of statistics but you should be able to produce substantial and authentic word-pictures of your teaching.

Adding such systematic evaluation to your more embedded lesson evaluation habits, and to your own intuitive experiences and responses, should help you to reach some conclusions about how lessons succeed and fail. Of course, we are talking here about fundamentals. A successful lesson is one where learning happens; and a failure is one where it doesn't. Issues of your performance, or of behaviour management, aren't of themselves significant evaluation focuses. Of course, they matter a lot; but they are subsidiary; they matter as part of the analysis of the learning, not as issues in themselves. These conclusions need to move beyond the pragmatic, reaching to the patterns behind it.

Such work, as we've said, is good preparation for reading established theory. Most modern learning theory is based on constructivism, and you could now re-read the section in Chapter 4 in which the work of Bruner and Vygotsky is summarised with criminal brevity. Of course, reading summaries of this kind isn't a substitute for reading the original texts, and there are suggestions in the bibliography.

Teachers in staffrooms don't sit around at coffee-time discussing social constructivism. In my experience, staffrooms were theory-free zones; they were pragmatic places. In recent years, however, there have been exceptions to this. *Learning styles* (see Chapter 6) and its little brother, *VAK*, have become current in staffroom conversation. While there is certainly an emerging learning-styles backlash (Is it actually a learning theory? Is it researched-based? Is it scientific?) it is rewarding to see staffrooms and staff meetings turning their attention away from duty rotas and school uniform to the business of how pupils actually learn. Any such learning theory can be applied to your evaluation of past teaching and to your proposals for future development in your practice.

Teacher-researcher

Action research is a way of studying your practice to solve problems and identify strengths within it and so to enhance it. Of course, you are doing this all the time; you simply have to develop your natural curiosity and evaluation into a research system which will link it to CPD or to personal improvement. By doing this, you will find out about research methods and values; you will find out about your school and how to change it; and you will find out about your own abilities. You will also probably develop your skills of collaborative working and enjoy having events at work which require you to focus on and discuss issues which are important to you.

An action-research project may begin from a simple question which you want answered. This may be a question about your own work, or perhaps the work of your school. There are many such questions covering many areas. You could research school restructuring, or curriculum development. You can involve children in the research (while paying close attention to the ethical implications of this). A fairly common and fruitful area of research is in the relationships between policies and practice. In effect, you might be considering whether a national or school-based initiative is really playing in the classroom as it should be, or as it claims to be.

For example, the UK's *Every Child Matters* initiative has been the subject of much publicity and training. It was originated in the aftermath of a tragic case of appalling cruelty and its main intention was to bind together the agencies that deal with children so that purpose, focus and information were shared. Several years later I am still hearing on the radio accounts of terrible things happening to small children because one agency didn't talk to another. It's tempting to think that the *Every Child Matters* project, despite all the activity surrounding it, has failed.

But I don't know that. It may be that many more serious cases of abuse have been prevented. Research dispels glib, uninformed, impressionistic reactions. Is someone carrying out this research at national level?

But *Every Child Matters* happens in school, too. You could ask the research question – How is the initiative working? – at school level. You could even ask it at classroom level. It isn't a teaching-and-learning policy; but it intends to impact on children's lives in all contexts, and the classroom is a big context for most children. Has teaching in your school actually changed as a result? How does that look? (For example, we said in Chapter 4 that the simple introduction of more group discussion would enhance the *ECM* presence, even supporting the requirement for economic well-being.) This could form the basis of a piece of action research within your school. As a result of its findings, you could make recommendations about future development.

Research can link to theory. Let's consider social constructivism (see Chapter 4) as a starting point. Having read and discussed Bruner, Vygotsky and others on constructivism and social constructivism, you might decide that speaking and listening should be central to the teaching and learning policy of your school, or alternatively to your own work. Perhaps this is already school policy. Your action research begins by simply finding out whether or not it is as central as it should be. You would move on to decide what to do about it.

Extending practice: assessment for learning

We are returning now to some final thoughts about improving your classroom practice. *Assessment for Learning* (AFL) is a recent UK initiative which bears directly on your teaching. If you're an experienced teacher wanting to revitalise your work, AFL might be a good place to look. Your assessment practice might be over-settled, and having another think about what assessment is *for* is a way of shining a light on your teaching in general. The name of the initiative puts assessment in its place – it exists to support learning, not simply to judge or report on it. It has been embraced by many as a way of doing more creative and varied things with assessment (peer assessment, self-assessment, and so on) and, while this is a good thing, and certainly better than nothing, it really only works when you're clear about the essential link between assessment and pupils' progress, and how this is driving the choices you're making.

The process of 'marking' is in fact a complex mixture of activities with a range of functions and processes; it will help if you unpick this, and try to revisit some underlying principles. Let's consider some of these functions.

As a teacher, you assess to gather information about the standard of pupils' work, perhaps to compare it with national expectations or with other pupils in the school. You may have to publish such information and comparisons to a range of different audiences. Perhaps your colleagues require diagnostic information. Perhaps parents want to know how things are going. Perhaps the government or your employers want to know how your pupils are getting on. Perhaps pupils themselves want to understand their situation.

Apart from this formal assessment practice, which may well involve large-scale and formal processes such as benchmarking and the setting of targets for pupils as an aspect of whole-school policy, there is a range of informal, day-to-day assessment activity, based on activities we still tend to describe rather quaintly as *marking*. These are vital activities, not simply the building blocks of formal assessment, but arguably of learning itself. If the large-scale activities described above could be called largely *summative*, these smaller-scale marking activities may be thought of as largely *formative* (though in fact most assessment procedures have a vital and essential formative element). In fact, what AFL is telling us is that we don't assess simply in order to gather statistics or to quantify pupils' efforts; we assess (and this includes day-to-day marking) in order to enhance pupil learning. It might be interesting to look at your own marking practice in the light of this. When you mark a pupil's work, when (for example) you write a comment or correct an error, do you habitually check yourself: how is this helping his learning?

This isn't as obvious as it sounds. For example, it has implications for your correction of pupils' mistakes. It may be tempting to underline every error, but this is unlikely to focus on patterns or repetitions; nor will it (of itself) provide any remedy. Your job is to explain so that the error is unlikely to be repeated. AFL has implications for written comments, too. In fact, you might like to think of written comments as working at three levels – *assessive*, *developmental* and *engaged*.

An *assessive* comment makes a quality judgement, as in: 'Very good work, though the arguments about the role of Shylock are quite simplistic.' I see this kind of comment frequently. In terms of our single criterion – does it enhance learning? – it isn't wholly useless. It draws attention to what needs improving, though it offers no suggestion as to how it should be done.

A *developmental* comment builds on this: 'Very good work, though the arguments about the role of Shylock are quite simplistic. You should consider his reactions at the end of the court scene as well as at the beginning.' It's obvious that this is more enhancing. It offers practical suggestions for improvement. However, a strong teacher could graduate to the third, *engaged* level:

> Very good work, though the arguments about the role of Shylock are quite simplistic. You should consider his reactions at the end of the court scene as well as at the beginning. I like your comparisons with modern racism – would a production set in 1930s Germany be effective or distracting, do you think?

Here, you are actually involving yourself in the pupil's writing, offering a dialogue with him. I've seen this in pupils' work books – the teacher writes a question arising from the work, and the pupil writes a reply. Such a dialogue isn't common, but when it happens it can become more enhancing than the original piece of work.

This isn't only fuller and more helpful, it's actually different in kind to the other comments, because it involves itself with the content of the pupil's writing; it engages with his thought. This engagement, which can also be achieved orally by teacher response to discussion, is significant in several ways. It builds a relationship in which the teacher is much more than an assessor and the pupil (therefore) much more than a passive recipient of knowledge and judgement. It differentiates, of course. Most of all, it seeks to engage the pupil by respecting his opinions and contributions. This is likely to enhance and extend the pupil's learning.

It's also a predominantly positive comment. Consider your comments, or consider the three sample comments above. The first is mostly negative; the second is about half negative; the third is largely positive. Are you achieving at least parity between what the pupil will perceive as negative and positive? And do remember that what may be intended as developmental support can look very like criticism to an adolescent. You aren't an adolescent, but don't you (even so) get tired of feedback which only focuses on weaknesses or 'development areas'? Celebrating positive achievement ('I particularly like the way you...') and commenting explicitly on progress ('You are far better now at...') is not only good for morale and relationships but efficient in defining and building improvement in your pupils. All of this may seem fairly obvious, but in reality many teachers stop at the assessive or developmental level in their marking and it does seem to need a conscious effort to habitually move beyond it. Of course, it requires more work and you haven't time to always do it for everybody; but you could combine it with *differentiation by rotation*, as discussed in Chapter 6.

We are making the point that assessment drives learning. We

don't mean that tests set the agenda for the classroom; we mean that we plan appropriate lessons when we know what pupils are good at and what they need to do better.

It's worth reflecting on this simple *strengths/weaknesses* model. People are quite uncomfortable with the *weaknesses* part of it and usually rename *weaknesses* as *areas for development* or some such euphemism. I think we are right to be wary of this simple dichotomy but I don't think that the problem is solved by rebranding it.

The problem with *strengths/weaknesses* as a comment model is that it's not as balanced as it looks. *Weaknesses* is the stronger partner. Even if the teacher is fastidious about half-and-half, the pupil is likely to remember and react to the weaknesses. The criticisms bother us disproportionately; that's human nature. For us to feel complimented we need about 80 per cent positive feedback.

However, the problem goes deeper than pupil reaction and morale. Ultimately, the problem is that weakness preoccupies the teacher as well as the pupil. Consider comments at the developmental level. The most common formula is: 'You are good at A, but not so good at B. We must now work on B in the following ways...'. Of course, this is common sense, and often it's the right direction. Assessment is driving learning. But the AFL relationship doesn't have to be negative, and progression is unbalanced if it always is. How often do you see comments like this? 'You are good at A, but not so good at B. We will work on B later, but for the moment we will build on the strength that you have with A...' The AFL relationship demands that you build on strengths as well as remedying weaknesses. The pupil works particularly well with historical sources, or has a very strong sense of how to apply algebra to real life, or is advanced in the technical analysis of poetry or the grammar of German. It matters very much to the pupil's development (not just to his morale) that these individual abilities are recognised and extended in your marking and the planning that flows from it. In this way your work is strongly differentiated and is likely to take pupils to new levels of sophistication within areas of strength. *To sum up: they need to move forward in areas of strength as well as areas of weakness.*

There is in fact a wide range of assessment practice, and perhaps it's time to think about moving beyond 'marking'. For example, there is self-assessment. You may encourage pupils to keep logs of their own experiences in your subject, perhaps writing responses to your marking comments, setting themselves targets to address as a result, marking and reflecting on their own work. A very interesting practice is to have the pupil mark her own work first. She may grade it according to relevant criteria (which have been explained to the whole class) and she will comment on its strengths and weaknesses. Then she will submit it for teacher-marking, without her grade or comments. Later she will be able to compare her marking with yours.

Peer-marking can be used on its own or combined with other processes such as self-marking or teacher-marking. Pupils need to be given clear criteria for marking each other's work, and to be reminded about positivity and development. It's certainly true that they will find things to say that teachers don't. Some research indicates that pupils will in fact be more critical than teachers are. This is also certainly true of self-assessment (and this includes the self-evaluation of teachers who are usually their own severest critics). So it's clear that a range of assessment types is likely to provide rich, varied and balanced information. As you develop, you will extend your assessment repertoire. But you must remember always its fundamental purpose, its fundamental connection with learning. You begin your lesson planning by knowing what pupils are good at and where they need to go next.

Development workshop revisited

In the opening chapter of this book we considered a series of continua – a chart of the journeys you might need to make to build your practice. In conclusion, I want to return to some of these journeys. If you've read the whole book, or if it's some time since you read Chapter 1, now is the time for you to consider whether you're moving forward in any of these areas.

I'm presenting this re-evaluation as a series of synoptic questions. They are grouped according to the continua, but they also have chapter references, so that you can explore further. I hope that, rather than barracking you with things you haven't done, this list reassures you that you've made some progress in two or three areas (more than that would be asking a lot in this timescale); and that it provides you with a few more questions to answer in the next few months. Don't try to cover everything. Like your pupils, you need to select, focus and concentrate; and you need to be positive and generous in your estimate of what's realistically possible.

Table 8.1

From 'limited activity' to 'inclusive differentiation'	
	Chapters
Are you planning individual lessons?	1,2
Are you planning from learning objectives?	1,2
Are you showing interest in pupils' reactions?	1,3,4
Are you constructing lessons with the pupils' interests and experiences in mind?	1,2
Are you remembering what it's like not to understand?	1,2
Are you remembering what it's like not to be interested?	1,2
Are you planning triadically?	2
Are you planning with a sense of pupils' attitudes and prejudices?	2
Are you thinking about the language of your subject?	2,4,6
Are you planning for choice?	4,6
Are you planning for creativity?	4
Are you scaffolding?	4
Are you using oral drafting?	4
Are you using children as experts?	4,5
Are you planning explicitly around EAL?	4
Have you read *A Language in Common*?	4
Are you being genuinely interactive?	5
Are you developing an inclusive view of differentiation?	6
Do you realise how much differentiation you already do?	6
Do you collaborate with Teaching Assistants?	6
Are you differentiating by rotation?	6
Do you use your language to differentiate?	4,6
Are you using learning styles?	6
Are you offering multiple access routes to the learning?	6
Are you allowing the able to challenge your lesson structures?	6
Are you encouraging the able to synthesise and extrapolate?	6
Are you encouraging children to think about the learning?	6
Are you stepping back to the fundamental questions?	6
Are the children encouraged to set tomorrow's learning objectives?	6,7
From 'activity-based planning' to 'objective-based planning'	
Are you thinking explicitly about your lessons?	1
Are you planning imaginatively and flexibly?	2,5
Are you using constructivist approaches?	2
Are you staging your learning objectives?	2,5
Are you writing local and specific learning objectives?	2

Table 8.1 continued

	Chapters
Are you recognising the central importance of transitions?	3,4,5,7
Are you moving towards the focus, not backing away from it?	3,4
Are you using DARTs appropriately?	4
Are you thinking about cross-curricularity?	4,5
From 'subjective evaluation' to 'systematic evaluation'	
Are you reflecting and evaluating systematically?	1,3,7,8
Are you involving pupils in evaluation and planning?	3
Is your evaluation focused on the three key questions?	7
Are you evaluating lessons at three levels?	7
Are you varying your evaluation methods?	7
Are you giving the plenary your full planning attention?	7
Are you responding to evaluations at two levels?	7
From 'administrating the lesson' to 'teaching the lesson'	
Are you planning to teach the lessons rather than administrate them?	1
Are you using examples, analogies and parallels in your explanations?	2,4
Are you using metaphors, similes and contrasts in your explanations?	2,4
Do you QDO when task setting?	3,4
Are you starting on the foothills?	3
Are you focusing on your own language?	4
Are you using examples?	4
Are you preparing and managing speaking and listening?	4
Are you trying for dynamic balance?	5
Are you being eventful as well as sustained?	5
Are you planning yourself and your words into the lesson?	5
Are you allowing yourself to be an expert?	5
Are you thinking about how pupils read?	4
Are you helping with note making?	4
Are you thinking of audiences for their speaking and writing?	4
Are you planning and teaching creatively?	1,5
From 'extrinsic behaviour management' to 'intrinsic learning management'	
Are you relating pupil behaviour to the planned work?	1,3
Are you explaining *why* the work matters?	1,3
Are you placing comparison at the heart of your teaching?	1,5
Are you planning for enjoyment?	2
Are you giving them a reading focus *before* reading?	4

Table 8.1 continued

	Chapters
Are you using familiar contexts to frame unfamiliar material?	2
Are you thinking about behaviour as you plan?	3
Do you use rewards and sanctions to explicitly depersonalise behaviour issues?	3
Are you being pro-active in planning for good behaviour?	3
Are you planning lessons which create a need to learn?	3
Are you understanding that *definition* isn't synonymous with *learning*?	3
Are you planning lessons with a clear story?	3,4
Are you planning openings very carefully?	3
Are you aware of the lesson subtext?	3
Do you understand stirring the tea?	3
Do you explain what sort of questions you're asking?	3
Do you avoid YAVA?	3
Do you have speaking and listening at the heart of your classroom?	3,4
Do you plan for SFC?	1,3
Are you planning opinion and prediction into your work?	3
Are you valuing and sharing difficulty?	3
Are you using jotting and thinking time?	3
Are you using group discussion roles?	4
Are you using text-type structures which the children already know?	4
Are you using prompt scripts and other planned lesson devices for focus?	5
Are you revitalising the coursework?	5
Are you moving from concrete to abstract?	5,6
Are you creating a secure, experimental classroom?	5
Are you building on pupils' strengths as well as their weaknesses?	8

From 'teacher' to 'teacher-researcher'

Are you thinking about CPD?	8
Are you arranging CPD that will combine with your existing workload?	8
Are you reviewing your practice explicitly?	8
Should you start a portfolio?	8
Is your portfolio focused?	8
Do you have composite portfolio evidence?	8
Does your portfolio tell a story?	8
Is your reflection analytical?	7,8

Table 8.1 continued

	Chapters
Are you returning (however briefly) to theory?	4,8
Should you undertake some action research?	8
Are you broadening your assessment practice?	8
Are you linking assessment to learning?	8
Are you making engaged and positive comments about pupils' work?	8

Suggested reading

Black, P. and William, D.: *Inside the Black Box* (Nelson).

Bruner, J.: *Towards a Theory of Instruction* (Norton).

Clarke, S.: *Formative Assessment in the Secondary Classroom* (Hodder).

Gardener, H.: *Multiple Intelligences: New Horizons in Theory and Practice* (Basic Books).

Ginnis, P.: *The Teacher's Toolkit* (Crown House).

Hubbard, R. and Power, B.M.: *Living the Questions: A Guide for Teacher-Researchers* (Stenhouse).

Kyriacou, C.: *Essential Teaching Skills* (Thornes).

Mills, G.: *Action Research: A Guide for the Teacher-Researcher* (Prentice Hall).

QCA: *A Language in Common*, online: www.qca.org.uk/qca_5739.aspx.

Vygotsky, L.S.: *Thought and Language* (Cambridge).

Wragg, E.: *Classroom Management* (Routledge).

Wragg, E.: *Classroom Teaching Skills* (Routledge).

Index